IDEALISM

THE ART OF EXALTING MAN

DARIN PENZERA

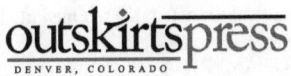

DENVER, COLORADO

Table of Contents

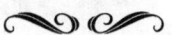

Part one—
Can I write?

1

Introduction—
The Key to Greatness

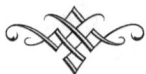

The journey begins—In opening this book you the artist have chosen to go on a journey to the realization of your creative potential. The path to greatness is there before you but the gates to it are locked, and what is needed is the key which will unlock the gate which will open up the path to greatness. To continue the quest we must find the key to greatness.

Great writers when they arrive are not lucky accidents. In the field of human greatness there are no lucky accidents. A great writer is not the result of being blessed by a divine power, not a result of being born with an innate talent, not a product of the environment, it is the end result of his making it to be so. *All great writers are self-created. All forms of human greatness are self-created.* The key to literary greatness, or any form of greatness, already lies within each man, and greatness is unlocked whenever a man decides to believe in himself.

The key to understanding my belief that anyone can be a great writer is this—writing is a *rational process,* therefore it is a field that can be *mastered by any rational man.* These two basic truths once realized and accepted will give you the key to unlock your potential for greatness.

Greatness is the result of a *way* of thinking. It is in how you think that determines your greatness or its lacking. Since you can think anything you want and change what you have been thinking you have the potential for greatness within you. We all have the potential for greatness within us. All you must do to start the journey to greatness is think greatness is possible to me.

Writing is not a field closed to all but a mystically endowed elite or the lucky few; literary greatness is not a lucky chance of birth or environment. Anyone with a normal functioning mind already has within them the means needed to produce superior literary works. Anyone willing to think and think hard will create great art. Anyone who believes in their potential will realize it.

To begin your journey to literary greatness you must first open up to a belief in yourself, *for self-belief is the key that unlocks the human potential. You can choose to be a great writer.* In saying yes to greatness, in the key of self-affirmation, the gate swings open and before you lies the path to the realization of your potential.

Belief in oneself is the spark which ignites the human will. To understand the true nature of the human will unleashed bring to your mind the image of fire. Fire is the unleashing of energy, uncontrolled it will destroy everything in its path; when rationally guided it reshapes even the hardest of things into the form the mind who can control the fire desires. See the fire in a steel mill, causing the running of molten steel, burning hot enough to incinerate any man who it touches, yet the liquid steel is channeled benevolently by the human will into the form it desires. This image of molten steel being created and moved by fire is the physical image of what is happening to the human potential inside a person who believes in themselves. The human will when ignited is also a fire but unleashing a far greater energy than any physical fire, for what is being unleashed is the spiritual energy of man. The human will once ignited creates a fire which melts away all resistance and channels the human potential down into the form it desires. Once belief gets ignited it becomes a roaring fire before which nothing can stand.

From the igniting the belief in your potential and the resulting burning will to realize that potential is the forge from which all human greatness emerges. If will is the fire belief is what ignites it. The mind molds itself, its fire and will lie within it. The mind is molded by what it thinks, and it is free to think whatever it wants. All greatness begins in the mind that realizes it can think its way to greatness and once believing this will forge greatness from its thoughts. The moment someone believes they have the potential for greatness they will immediately begin to act to realize their potential. Once a person believes it can be so they will go about making it so, and the quest begins and continues until they have made belief reality.

All great writing begins in the mind, in a mind that both believes it can write and seeks and finds *how* to think about writing. All you have to do to be a great writer is learn to approach your writing through the right mindset or philosophy for writing. To be a great writer all you must do is teach your mind to think in the right ways. To be a great writer all you must do is think like a great writer thinks.

The ideal expressed here on the cause of literary greatness places me completely at odds with the opposite school of theory on what produces literary greatness, the deterministic school.

The deterministic school holds that talent is not earned but granted; talent is not a potential cultivated it is given complete, given through some means without any effort on the part of the writer. Within the deterministic school of thought there are broadly speaking three prevailing ideas on how men are granted their talent, the lucky birth belief, the lucky environment belief and the divine power belief. The lucky birth theorist holds that a writer is born with the talent, the lucky recipient of the right genes. The lucky environment theorist holds that a writer's talent is the result of him being in the right place. The divine power theorist holds that a superior or divine power grants to men their talent. Or a variation on the divine inspiration theory is that a superior power does not give a man his talent once and for all but grants it to men at times when it wants them to write well, talent on divine loan so to speak. Regardless of how they came to the idea for the determinist talent and human greatness are not earned through the rational efforts of men. To the determinist thru no actions of your own you are predestined to being great, or greatly untalented. The sum belief of determinism is either you already have the talent or else you do not.

The fundamental difference between the two schools is the rational man strives to realize something the determinist expects to already be realized. One says your talent has to be realized, the other says it is already realized or if not it can never be realized.

Determinism is invalidated by this simple fact—man is a *rational being*. Man has no automatic knowledge, who must choose both to think and what to think, who may think and choose what to think as he wishes, who can choose *through his own efforts* to intellectually labor to acquire the knowledge he needs, where the genesis of talent and greatness lies in the man who realizes this truth, and through his own efforts learns to use his mind in the right ways for the right ends, who acquires his skills and talents by repeatedly acting in the right ways upon the right knowledge, who does this because he believes he can, because he believes he is man the rational being. This metaphysical fact of human existence, that man thinks, invalidates all the theories of the determinist.

The consequences of believing in determinism leads to this happening to the potential artist and his potential, either 1—the artist does not put in the time to develop his potential, and/or 2—he puts in the time but does not use the tools or ideas that will actually develop his potential. These reasons are why those who believe in determinism fail to realize greatness.

Those determinist who fail to put in the time do so because they believe it is not necessary, determinist that they are believe putting in massive amounts of time practicing their art will make no difference, for their talent is already there for better or for worse. Putting in no time to develop their talent their talent never develops.

Those who put in the many hours in their art but are not dedicated to employing the proper tools of thought, to ensure their thoughts are proper, determinist that they are believe it is not necessary to retool the mind for the tools are already built into the mind, and failing to develop the right tools of thought their potential is never built into anything.

Writing like any skill takes time and effort to learn. Those who assume that writing talent is given when they first begin to write and see that their writing is not of a superior quality (as everyone will be in the beginning) they logically assume they lack the talent and so throw down their pen in frustration, believing they have not been blessed with talent. The joke is on them though, the potential talent is there, and could be unlocked if only they believed in themselves and their ability to cultivate their potential.

No great artist started out as being so. Even Shakespeare in the beginning was not Shakespeare. (Shakespeare the revered artist.)

You either have it or you do not is a false belief. You either cultivate the potential talent you have or else you do not.

One of the most important things you need to realize about acquiring talent is that it is an *evolutionary process*. Acquiring talent is something you build up as an everyday affair, it is acquired and increased a little every day; like a skyscraper talent is not built in a day but goes up one story at a time. A person to become great must everyday in his field push himself further than he did before, acquiring knowledge, learning new techniques, perfecting old ones, learning the ins and outs of the trade, and over time this constant expanding of his talent causes it to grow to a truly great height.

No singer sings for the first time expecting to reach an operatic range. No painter touches the canvas for the first time expecting to produce a Sistine Chapel. No sculptor strikes the marble for the first time expecting to sculpt a statue of David. Only writers for some reason think they can put pen to paper for the first time and produce a masterpiece.

Talent is not given it is acquired. While we are all given a potential without effort it is up to each one of us to choose to make the effort to realize our potential. While it is true we all may not start building on the same level it is necessary for everyone to build up their talent in order to reach the heights of their full potential.

The rational writer takes the time and the effort to learn the principles of writing and the even more difficult task of learning how to make them a part of him. The determinist believing the talent is already within them fails to make the effort.

This is how determinism destroys the human potential, it leaves men without the *spark of belief and the resulting fire of will* needed to shape the human potential. What talent needs is the time to be realized, by following the right ideas thru the time needed to fully realize them. Only belief in oneself enables one to travel thru all the effort and time needed to forge something of oneself. Belief is what unleashes the human flame that forges the human potential. Lack of belief in our potential and our ability to shape it snuffs out the human flame.

The writer who does write from a deterministic philosophy believing that since talent is given he does not approach his writing with a system for cultivating his talent. He does not have any fire within to shape the potential within him. He does not have any writing principles that will lead him to greatness because his theory is that literary greatness cannot be rationally forged. He does not seek any idea of how to create great works of art, doing so because he holds the belief that everything he needs to do so should already be given to him. The determinist writer is the one who has no system for writing, and so he writes from blindness, his writing a groping in the dark for the way, no way to determine if he is going the right or wrong way, no standard to judge good or bad, no standard to say this is how you write. Without a system to guide him he writes in the dark and his writing ends up lost. He then loses the fire to write because he believes he lacks the talent to write.

The rational writer creates his own fire and molds himself in its heat. Right thought followed by right effort is his working motto. His working motto unleashes his full potential, the only real potential and power man has, his thoughts and the power to determine which thoughts he will hold. He does not believe that talent is a matter of luck but cultivates the potential talent he has, making his own luck. He does not passively wait hoping his environment will shape him he creates the environment in which he shapes himself. He does not wait for an outside power to tell him what to write about or how to write it, he uses his own rational powers. The rational writer unleashes his powers by always approaching his writing in a state of *rational seeking*; he learns *what* he wants to write and *how* he should do it. The rational writer becomes the great writer because he works long and hard, working long and hard to embody the principles of greatness; he becomes great because he thought his way to and used the methods of thought that produce greatness.

Only a writer who believes he can cultivate his potential has the potential to produce literary greatness. The determinist are doomed to defeat, not by the nature of circumstances or divine will but through the nature of their own actions, that of abdicating the source of all human greatness, putting fully to use the potential of your mind.

The desire of the determinist is perhaps a desire for an automatic unerring form of knowledge. The philosophy of the determinist is really an expression of a desire for the *unearned*. The determinists express a desire not to have to work to develop their potential but to just have it developed already. Since man has no automatic unerring form of knowledge, since he needs to acquire knowledge through his own efforts this is why the determinist writers are always stalled and doomed for failure, because they are waiting for an inspiration or knowledge that will never come.

More likely if we probe into the deeper *psychological* truth with some of the determinist is that their claimed belief in determinism is held not as a belief but as a *rationalization*, an attempt to create a psychological escape clause from the self-knowledge that one is a failure. A man who desires to be a great but refuses to make the effort to become so resorts to the determinist theory to rationalize his failure to himself. "Well I would be great if only God/circumstances/luck had favored me as it favored others" so he says to himself to soothe a shaken self-esteem. Perhaps we have given the advocates of this theory a belief in their sincerity that most do not deserve, assuming sincerity where only rationalization and lying is going on.

Determinism besides being a false belief is also a dangerous belief. (Dangerous to the *sincere* determinist.) The belief that talent is given has probably done more to destroy so many potentially good writers and more human potential than any other false belief. There is no way to calculate how much potential talent has been destroyed by the theory of determinism, what I do know is that enough has been destroyed by this false theory to make it worth the effort to destroy it.

What may have worked to contribute to the elitist view in writing is that great writers are admittedly a rarity, and this is because so very few men truly believed in themselves and acted on that belief. The rarity of real literary talent works to make men think it is a unique gift rather than a commonly held trait. When the literary greats do arrive they seem blessed, for we hold the end result of their efforts which seems to have come naturally and effortlessly, yet this is because we seeing only the end result cannot see the *process* of thought and effort that went into producing the mind and mindset capable of producing such literary works. A process we can all undertake.

The process of becoming a good writer is a process of learning to hold the right ideas. We all hold the potential to be good writers for we all hold the potential to hold the right ideas.

Do not wait for the lightning bolt of inspiration to strike you; do not wait for a thunderous voice of divine will to tell you the way; learn how to create your own lightning bolts of inspiration, learn how to speak in your own thunderous voice.

In seeking to create greatness do not look outward, do not stand idly by, journey into yourself, spark the fire within and in it forge your potential until it assumes the form of greatness.

The great in any field know their path is not predetermined; the great determine their own path, and are determined to be great and act until it becomes so.

No man begins any project unless he believes he has the tools to build what he wants and believes he knows how to use those tools. So long as belief in yourself is lacking even if you have every other tool needed you will fail, for the tools lie useless before a paralyzed mind. Belief empowers the mind and will, and they once empowered grasp the tools needed to do what they desire to do. Believe in yourself and here is forged the key which unlocks everything else you will need.

The seed of greatness already lies within you, in your *reasoning* mind, and if you believe this you will take the seed of that potential and cultivate it until it flowers into greatness. Just believe greatness lies within you and you will have unlocked your potential and the journey to make it grow into greatness will begin and continue until greatness is arrived at.

Writing is one of the noblest activities and greatest joys a man can engage in. This is because writing when done under the right premises is an expression of pure rationality, a man expressing the highest that is possible to him. Writing when it is guided by the right ideas and ideals it is man living up to the highest potential of his nature. The principles and practices, ideas and ideals that follow in this book are the tools out of which you will forge literary greatness.

On the form of this book

The form of this book stands as a guide, a mentor to all those on their hero's journey to realize their potential. Like the wise old man standing on the mountain peak holding the light we can all look up to him and be guided by the light of the mentor to the heights.

In the pages that follow is outlined a system for writing, a series of writing principles which will serve as guides on your journey towards producing great literary works. These principles will tell you what to write about and how to write it. First is defined the ultimate purpose of all worthwhile writing, for this gives to you a literary mark for your pen to aim for. Here the peak is spotted and marked as the goal. In the following chapters is defined the means of style and execution, specific writing principles designed to allow you to hit your literary mark. Here the tools are given to scale the heights. These principles if followed sincerely and consistently will guide you successfully through the whole process of literary creation, allowing you to hit the high mark every time.

There is a method to properly produce literary art. (Or anything.) Strip art of its mystical mumbo-jumbo and we will be able to see its core truth that all great art was produced by a man who acted on the right methods for producing great art. Guiding your writing by a series of principles for guidance is simply defining the methods that actually work for producing what you want. Having a system of principles for writing means you know the end you desire and the best means to get you there. Having a system for writing is having made the intellectual effort to train your mind to think in the right ways about writing.

Many great artists arrive at the way thru stumbling, thru a vast amount of trial and error, a continual series of accidents unto they fall upon the right principles for writing, and oftentimes they do not fully realize or articulate the principles, so even after they find they way they often lose it again, their journey to greatness a long, meandering one, with a lot of wrong turns and lost time. In this writing manual it defines a clear cut destination and lays out a map to guide you there, so your journey will be a relatively straight line, without the continual stumbling, massive trial and error, and repeated accidents that are the usual winding roads of so many others journey to greatness. If you are lost this manual is the map showing the way.

Merely reading this book will not make you a great writer. This book can only serve as a guide on the way, you must travel the way. The process of transforming your mind's ways of thinking is one only you can do, but it is a process that takes time. Teaching someone to write is similar to teaching them to swim, you can explain to someone how to swim but they will never be able to do it until they actually dive in and start swimming. If you want to learn to swim then you must actually dive in and swim, yet there are better and worse ways of swimming, and proper instruction can guide you to employing and cultivating your potential better. It is easy enough thru thinking to see the right idea but it is far more difficult to make the right idea a part of your *way* of thinking. Reading this book will not automatically make you a great writer. You must dive in and start writing, and while writing apply the principles outlined in this book sincerely and consistently to your writing, using the book as a way to guide your own efforts, applying the principles offered until they become a part of you and then you will have self-created yourself into a great writer.

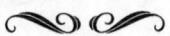

Part two—
Why Should I write?

2

The Spell of Writing

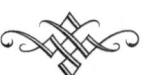

If magic is the power to transform reality thru the spell of words then writing is truly a magical power. The writer with the pen as his wand, using the incantatory power of words, can cast a spell over an individual, or even the whole world.

In the word spelling is the root word spell—when spelling a word you are literally casting a spell. To write is to attempt to cast a spell over a reader. A series of words when written and read in the right way can be magic for they can literally change people and reality. Words are magical symbols whose ability to enchant are a truly transformative power. The magical power of writing once read can transform people, raise up or bring down whole societies, reorder the world, change the course of a life or all human history.

Good writing casts a memorizing spell on us. We have all had those reading experiences were the writer cast a spell on us, where for a time we left this world and entered their world, traveled in it, and came back to this world transformed by the magical experience.

Bad writing too casts the spell, the spell of revulsion or boredom upon the reader. Words can wield great power both ways.

Writing transcends the normal human limits of space—Writing gives to you a voice which can heard by the whole world. Writers have a voice whose distance is measured not in feet but across the distance of a universe.

Writing transcends time—A writer's words unlike the spoken word live on beyond the moment, his words a magical force defying time, living thru time, becoming timeless. A writer's words can be a thunder which echoes thru all time.

Writing transcends even death—The writer in successfully committing the spell of words to paper is to create something that will live on long after he is dead and even his dust has been lost to the winds. The writer's words become living beings, the writer still living on thru those words, and still affecting the living with those words. Thru writing even death can be transcended. Writing gives to one the power to defy death. Writing gives to mortal men an immortal power.

Writing makes what was invisible visible—A few words can make us see what was long hidden to us. Particularly words unlock the human spirit, the greatest repository of secrets, often the hardest to crack open, yet the right words easily unlock it.

Writing holds the power to heal—Words, which can magically transform the physical world, can also transform the spiritual as well. Words can touch a man at his very core. Words can heal the human spirit, put the shattered human back together. Words can also hurt the human spirit, shatter the whole person. Indeed words have their most immediate and also most lasting effect within the human spirit.

Writing can transform the world around us—The writer has the power to enchant the world around us, or enchant us with the world. The writer can make the mundane the spectacular, transform everything into objects of beauty, bring wonder to all the known world.

Writing has the power to transport us—A literary work can be a portal to a heaven or a hell. A writer thru words can spiritually move the human soul. Moving words move the soul somewhere. The writer must carefully choose his words so he can move souls to a place worth being moved to.

The writer possessing a magical power like all those with power of some kind can use his powers for good or evil. The writer must realize how much his words can affect his time and the time beyond his time. Words holding so much power can be used for good or evil, to give joy or pain, to heal or injure, to give life or to take it. In casting the spell of writing the writer must begin with a respect for the power of words. A writer to be a force for good must know the proper goal for using such a power.

3

Idealism—
Art That Exalts Man

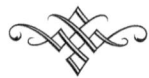

Art is a moral crusade to raise man to his proper place in the world. Here with this proclamation I launch my campaign to make the goal of art a holy one, to make the artist a holy warrior, to make the artist mission a divine mission.

All worthy crusades begin by rallying the troops around a worthy idea. Crusades are fought in the name of ideas. Moral crusades are fought for the right ideas. This is a crusade fought to at last give artists the right idea about art's *moral goal and purpose*. Crusades have been fought before in the realm of art, over style, over rules of grammar, over many other miniscule things, yet here this crusade seeks to change the whole *moral aim* of the field of art as such.

This crusade is fought for an idealistic role for art, so let this artistic crusade be called idealism. Here I raise an exalting banner over the field of art so at last artists have a banner worth following in the battle for art's meaning. Banners represent spiritual ideas raised up high. This exalted banner will raise the right idea up high and rally the faithful to the highest cause art can serve.

Upon this banner is emblazoned three symbols—moral goal, purpose, spirit, the three core elements of art. Moral goal is what art is supposed to achieve for and within man. Purpose is what the art itself is supposed to achieve. Spirit is the moral sum of fulfilling the purpose of art. The banner of idealism followed faithfully will lead the art and artist to the heights of artistic triumph and glory.

The decision made to create art as the purpose of your life the life changing decision process is only half-complete, the question still remaining is what kind of artist are you going to be? What kind of artistic standard are you going to follow? What kinds of stories do you want to tell? What kind of humans do you want to depict? What kinds of ideals do you want to set forth on your pages? What kind of ideal of life do you want to make your books add up to? Are you going to glorify heroes or scoundrels? Uplift or denounce man? Glorify achievement or damn it? Are you going to depict life as good or show it as being a sewer of depravity and pain? Is the spirit of your books going to be the exalting yes to life or the resounding no to it? To write literary works of worth you must first have a worthy standard to be led by. Literary greatness begins by knowing to write about that which is worth writing about. Great art is never an accident; great art emerges only when the artist created according to the standards of great art. Only by following the exalting banner of idealism will you have the standards which will lead your writing and yourself to greatness.

Here I raise my artistic banner, the standard of idealism—

Moral goal—*The moral goal of art is to exalt man in spirit. Art's goal is to be the wings which uplifts the human spirit.* Great art creates or reinforces a life-affirming spirit within man, taking him up the point where he says yes, *this* is worth living for.

Purpose—*The purpose of art is to show what man and his life can be and should be.* (Should be meaning the highest humanly possible.) *Art maps out the realm of highest possibility.*

Art achieves its purpose by projecting the pursuit and achievement of meaningful human values, the values which make man and his life into what it should be, something great, something worth living for. Art must show the proper values of a human life and in doing so shows the value of human life. Art's purpose is to be a light which illuminates values to man, illuminating to man his own value.

Spirit—The spirit of art is or should be possessed by an exalted feeling for man and his life, to add up thru the sum of the art the sense that man and life *are good*. The spirit of art should add up to a symphony that celebrates the goodness of human life. The ultimate spiritual sum of idealism is it is art that is *life-affirming*.

The dictionary definition of idealism—1—To show a standard of excellence or perfection in artistic form, 2—to show the nature of a meaningful idea, 3—to be visionary, to show what *could* be, 4—to uphold a model for imitation, a goal to aim for, 5—to treat subjects imaginatively (as opposed to realism), 6—to exalt the subject in representation—these are the dictionary definitions of idealism, and they all add up to my ideal of art, the ultimate sum of which is to show man and his life as they could be and should be, meaning in their highest state.

The highest purpose art can assume, 1—to show an ideal human being living the ideal life or 2—to show how to become the ideal human being living the ideal life. The sum of the highest and greatest art always *shows the values of the ideal human and the value of the ideal human*. Art exalts man in spirit when it shows him the exalted peak of the ideal human living the ideal life and/or the way to climb to it.

To approach your writing guided by the principle of idealism means the glorification of the good man and life through your writing, whether it be fiction or non-fiction. The goal of idealistic fiction is to show man at his best; in idealistic non-fiction the goal is to show the principles that motivate the best of men.

Idealism literature's method is both depictional and instructional, to show man's greatness and to show how to achieve it within yourself. Idealism both enlightens and inspires. Idealism projects man's highest aspirations and becomes the stairway to their realization.

The worthy artistic banner is inscribed with these ideals—moral goal—to exalt man in spirit, purpose—to show what man and his life can be and should be, spirit—to show man and life as good, the sum of this banner I call idealism. (Idealism because its concern is with the achievement of the highest that can be both within the literary work and within the spirit of man.)

What is a value? Anything of *great value* to the *great man*: virtue, heroism, adventure, creation, art, culture, friendship, romance, freedom, happiness. Here the artist to create art of value must first seek the *ideas* of what are values. The artist must first be a philosopher. First must be found the ideas, then the way (style) to present them.

Here I seek to rejoin in a holy union two long separated disciplines, art and philosophy. The philosopher's job is to seek ideas; the artist's job is to present ideas. What is the artist who is not a philosopher? Someone who will end up using words but without saying much of anything. What is the philosopher who is not an artist? He who may have ideas but his words will not move men thru his writings to his ideas.

Art is not an end in itself, only man is an end in himself. Art to be of value must serve man and serve him well. The enlightenment, elevation and exaltation of man is the moral purpose of art. For all good writers are also philosophers, lovers of wisdom enlightening the mind for the ultimate purpose of uplifting the human spirit. In uplifting the spirit of man this also makes the writer a religious crusader.

The idealist artist makes his art a form of religion, a religion dedicated to exalting human beings, his work a bible for humanity, the result of a religious worship of man. To open up a work of idealism art is to open up the gates that show the way to heaven. The idealistic writer does not talk like a man when he talks to other men; he speaks like a God when he talks to men. A God does not speak of the mundane or depraved; he speaks only of divine things, and speaks in a way worthy of the subject being discussed.

Life to be made high and exalted requires man to pursue and achieve the highest human values; art's purpose is to show men *what* values to pursue, *how* to pursue them and above all else *why* they should pursue them. To show what life becomes for those who pursue and achieve the highest values is the best means to show men why they should pursue the high values of life.

Art is a beacon, a light shining forth in the darkness. Art is the light shining upon some value of human existence. The greatest most worthy art shines like a great sun illuminating the greatest and most exalted of human values.

To fulfill the proper spirit of art in showing what man and his life can be this does not mean the artist has to show a world where every value has already been realized but to show a world where humans are living up to or embodying or realizing their own highest values, and realizing their own value, humans acting as they should be in a world being made into what it should be. Worthwhile art often shows man and his life in a process of transformation and shows this process as an uplifting one.

Art should be the domain of the idealistic, for those who see things not as they are but as they should be. As the average writers articulate truths we all see it is the great writers who articulate truths no one sees. The goal in being idealistic is not to show man and life as it is but to show man and life as it could be and should be, in order to say *this* is what is possible to *you*. For the artist to assume an uplifting meaningful role he must be an idealist in spirit because such a spirit breaks the dreary chains of what is and gives him the wings to soar to the heaven of what can be. In entering the idealistic world of art the artist is no longer bound by this world as it is or humans as they are but instead can create the world and humans as he wants it to be. This is the great freedom and power and joy of art, that the artist becomes the human equivalent of a God, able to make man and the world as he wills it.

Art is a flight into fantasy. Art to be a flight worth taking must take off with idealistic wings for only such wings take us to a fantasy worth being in. The artist creates an artistic fantasy world, a world where we can lose ourselves in the land of his ideas; the goal in losing yourself in an artwork is not to escape from life but to at last find life as it should be. The artistic flight into alternate realities is taken not as a means to escape from this reality but to ultimately return to this reality armed with the spiritual and intellectual tools needed to live successfully in this reality.

The exalting idealist artist method—to create ideal humans and place them up high, in order that we will look up and grasp the highest conception of what man can be, and grasp the belief in man's greatness, to come away exalted in spirit because we also grasped the belief that such greatness *is possible to us,* by grasping the idea of man's greatness in art we seeing such a high standard in art live up to that standard and grasp greatness in reality. The artist by providing man with heroic images and ideas his art becomes the wings which lifts man up to a higher conception of life.

The idealistic writer creates his artistic fantasy world, to transport himself and his readers to a place worth living in, a world overflowing with the highest human values, where on every page the great values of life and the value of life stands forth, where man is shown as good, where life is good, where man and his life are as they should be, all idealistically presented in a book overflowing with a passion for living life, because the goal of the idealistic writer is to give to those who read the work the same passion for life, and as we read our souls are infused with the same passion for what life can be, where we take this knowledge and use it to guide us in our own lives and become the better for it, but more than just a particular knowledge of some value we come away from such an artwork with the knowledge that *life itself is a value,* the knowledge that life as such is good makes us believe that life is worth living, and this belief makes us affirm the value of life leading us to the highest value of all, where we achieve *an exalted state of life,* and in this exalted heavenly moment the moral purpose of art is achieved.

The reader swept up into the alternate reality of the artistic world often finds himself upon returning to this world that this world was *transformed* in his absence. What has really changed is his view of the world. Art often gives us new eyes with which to see the world. What art does is not so much transform the world but transforms us in spirit and it is the transformed spirit which then physically transforms the world around it.

The spirit once transformed then acts to make the spiritual view a concrete reality. The exalting artist in artistic form shows us the highest life can be, and what life becomes for those who believe. Art both fuels and drives the human spirit. Art feeds the reader the idea of what he and his life can be, a fantasy that begins to drive him in reality, the reader feeding upon the spirit of the art says yes I can be this, my life can be this, here art begins achieving its moral goal, for the reader is transformed in this moment, he begins acting as the ideas and ideals of the art say he should, he and the world around him are transformed, fantasy and reality are now the same thing, life has become as it should be, here he does not just think life can be good *it is good*, here he exists in a complete state of life-affirmation, here the ultimate moral goal of art is most truly and completely fulfilled. Art by showing the values in life ultimately shows us the value of life. In showing the values in life and of life the artist recharges the soul for life. Just as the body must be fed to ensure physical survival so to must the spirit be fed to ensure spiritual survival. A soul can die starved of ideas. Ideas are the fuel of the soul. Books are the richest source for feeding hungry minds.

The exalting idealist goal—artistic creation not to kill time but to ensure we use our time wisely; not to allow our potential to waste away but to ensure we are being driven to the fulfillment of our potential; not a heroic standard detached from us but to ensure we attach ourselves to a heroic standard; not art divorced from life but art married to a higher ideal of life, art seeking to bring us into union with that life.

Art is not meant to be the means by which we escape from life but the means by which we learn how to fully immerse ourselves into it.

The artist provides mankind the ideas, ideals, symbols and slogans which will move it forwards and upwards. Art is the vehicle for taking man to higher places.

The artist assumes the role of being both visionary leader and inspiring preacher to mankind; to first realize within himself the highest ideal that can possibly be, and to then to articulate that ideal in artistic form, preaching to men that such an ideal is possible to them, moving men to the belief in themselves and moving them to realizing it in reality.

Art as a beacon showing the way to life, the highest life. The artist is a star who because of the way he shines down upon the world allows us to see the world in a whole new light.

IDEALISM—ART THAT EXALTS MAN

Art is the moral light of this world. Indeed it is when the world is in its darkest times that it cries out the loudest for the artist to save it. The darkness often falls because the artist was silent, or spoke darkly of this world. As the sun retakes the world from darkness so too must the artist aspire to be a blazing star who takes man from a world of darkness to a new dawn. When the idealist artist rules the day then the world moves thru a perpetual sunlit day.

All you really need to be a good writer is the right philosophy on life and the right philosophy for writing about life. The principle of idealism is the philosophical sum of two ideals, to express the ideal philosophy for man for living life thru an idealistic form of writing.

You become an idealist in spirit by allowing yourself to be possessed by an exalted view of man, allowing an overflowing of love and joy for what man can be to pour out of you and into the art, this achieved by 1—focusing on the highest that man can be and 2—presenting it in a way that appeals to the highest that is within man. You write about the good and you write about it in a way that shows you believe in the good, and you do it in the way you write as if you are addressing a good human being, i.e. you do it in a completely rational idealistic way.

The artist truly is a heroic figure. He moves man forwards and upwards. He provides the ideas and ideals for us to look up to, to live up to. He makes us realize more about ourselves, realize there is more about ourselves than we ever realized. The idealist artist creates the heroic ideal saying *this* is what is possible to *you*. Those who can see what the artist see realize this is possible to me. Before greatness can be realized in reality it must be realized that greatness is possible in reality.

The credo of any idealist artist—I will create the most heroic life-affirming art the world has ever seen. This is the highest ideal of the artist, the only worthy ideal for the artist.

Begin with a worthy enough why and you will find a way to achieve it. To write the fiery words that burn themselves into the soul the writer's soul must itself first be stoked with a fiery passion. The writer in writing must be passionate about what he is writing about and passion flows only from the belief that your reasons why are right and good. The clarity of knowing your why will eventually lead you to the how.

The following list is a conceptual map designed to lead you to a worthy why.

Why should I write?

The universal questions—the ultimate reasons why I want to write?
1—Why do I want to write?
2—What ideal or goal do I want my writing to aspire to?

The goal of art—to exalt man in spirit
The purpose of art—to show what man and his life can be and should be.
The spirit of art—to show man and his life as good.

A worthy reason why to write leads you to the right ideas to write about.

The questions of what to write?
1—What is it I want to write?
2—Why should I be the one writing it?

1—*What is it I want to write about?*
    1—What idea do I want to write about?
    2—Why is this idea worthy of being written about? (In what way will artistically depicting this idea fulfill the moral goal and purpose of art?)

2—*Why should I be the one writing about this idea?*
    1—What justifiable reason makes this idea worth writing about to me?
    2—What do I actually know about the idea and how to present it that makes me the person to be writing about it?

Know your why and the how will follow.

This map provides only a list of questions which each writer must make his own journey to his own worthy answers for. If you cannot come up with what is to you worthy answers to each of these questions then *do not write, until or unless the worthy answers are found.*

The other schools of writing—the trifling and depravity

This theory stated here as the goal of art being to show man as a being of greatness places me at odds with the other schools of thought on the goal of art, the trifling and depravity schools.

The three approaches in determining the kind of spirit your works will have are 1—idealistic (positive)—to show man at the best he can be, 2—depraved (negative)—to show man at the worst he can be, and 3—trifling (neutral)—to show an insignificant view of man, as man as being nothing much one way or the other.

Here I speak not of the form or style of a work but its essential spirit—what spirit of man and his life does the art show? The truly important question facing the artist is not what kind of literary setting are you going to put people in but what kind of people are you going to be putting in your literary settings. In most artworks an artist will present two or even all three views of man, yet the all important question is what view of man will the artist present as the *primary* importance, which one represents what most men are or should be or must be.

In the trifling genre the writer has no stand for or against man, no stand for or against higher values; the trifling artist stands for nothing. The depravity artist stands against every human value and every human and stands for everything humans should not be.

First we must tackle the trifling school of art. The word trifle is another word for insignificance, and this is the view of man such a school seeks to present, of man as a being of no real significance. This is presented in works which show man's actions and life adding up to nothing of significance.

The trifle school of art comes from a little view of man, that man is a being of little consequence, little importance, and so his art should reflect that. The main point of trifling art is that it has little meaning: little people in spirit, little stories with little at stake, little of consequence, all in order to show that life itself has little meaning, if it has *that* much. This art if it exalts anything exalts the common, the common man, a common life, Main Street, the folks next door. Such an art though does not exalt man.

This brings up the question, of what worth is art if it tells us what we do not care about? What we *should not* care about?

The trifling artist presents the little things of life, as if these are the highest meaning and essence of life. Ultimately people reading and accepting such things will feel as if life has little to no real meaning.

In reading a trifling artwork you will often say is this *all* life has to offer. You will feel if accepting the trifling artist viewpoint that life may not necessarily be bad yet it is not really great either.

Those reading such stories do not feel uplifted, and indeed if accepting the ideals of such art will feel no need to lift themselves up.

Trifling art is the art of the pleasant pasttime, a way to wile away the hours of life without being too aware that something so precious is being wasted away. Trifling art also performs an act of idealism diversion, it draws men away from pursuing the higher ideals of life; indeed the very desire to be relieved of the burdens of meaningful pursuits is often what causes people to go to trifling art.

Art that appeals to the insignificant man often does so because it justifies to him that it is all right that he is the insignificant man.

Trifling art does not seek to present high ideals and highflying heroes in pursuit of those ideals, for such art would give him his own wings to soar on, give man an *uplifted* sense of his potentiality. The trifling artist is he whose soul has no wings to uplift him.

Trifling artist do not hate man, indeed may even feel some warmth towards him, more likely amusement, but they lack a true love of man and his potential greatness. They do not necessarily damn man as a devil but they do not bless him as a divine being.

The trifling artist renounces his chance to be a God of magnificence, a creator of a magnificent glory, he is a God of banality, creating a mundane world, more so failing to show man how to be a magnificent God who creates a world of true glory.

To open up a trifling artwork is to open up a work that is a moral void. Trifling art is art without values or value; it is of no human value as it is divorced from concern for higher values, especially any concern for the highest human value—the ideal human.

A writer is often a shape shifter, taking from the real world persons, places, events, and placing altered versions of them in his work. The trifling artist ignores the extremes of men, ignores the highest and lowest of men and takes the average, the mundane, those not greatly good or evil either way. The idealistic artist often too uses the men around him for his work but only as a springboard to launch himself to a higher type of man, the average men remade into a divine image; the ultimate goal is to show men the way to remake themselves and their lives into that divine image. A trifling artist does not remake man in a divine image; he follows men paper and pen in hand and records the most mundane things he sees.

What is art? Art is creating a fantasy world whose elements are drawn from the real world. Why recreate the world around us in artistic form? The creation of a fantasy world is done to show us what is possible to us in the real world. To show a higher ideal of man and life, to say this is what is possible to you; *this* is why we need art, not to show us what is which we already can see but to show what can be which we often need art's help to see. The idealist remakes the artistic world in the image of his values, in order ultimately to remake the real world in the image of his values. The trifling artist is he who has no desire to remake reality into the image of his highest values, for he does not hold any real high values and his art shows it.

Trifling writing devoid of any sense of human greatness is one you could barely remember while reading and is forgotten about as soon as the book is put down. A book that fails to present or stand for anything truly worthwhile is a book made to be thrown away, that will be thrown away after being read and more so *should be* thrown away. Trifling writing ends up being a waste of paper. Many artists create throwaway art,

art deliberately designed to be read only to kill time and thrown away once enough time has been murdered by it. How low must an artist's self-esteem be to create works designed ultimately to be garbage?

The artist who aspires to be read and then forgotten deserves to be forgotten before he is read.

All good people yearn and strive for meaning and value in their lives. The trifling artist has lost this; he seeks not to give deep meaning to life but to escape from the need to give it meaning by immersing himself in the mundane and meaningless aspects of life. While deep meaning for life may be read into his works the trifling artist does not seek to write such meaning into it. Trifling art is hard to feel alive in while reading, as one is reading a work dead in spirit, for it is devoid of meaning, and all decent people yearn for meaning in art and life, and cannot for long endure a reading experience or a life completely devoid of it.

You bold and enterprising readers may say since the trifling may stumble upon and record meaningful human values or I can put meaning into his works I can enter the trifling world as a prospector for values; to this I say be very careful for the trifling world is one heavy with the gravity of indifference and your spirit could be crushed under this horrific weight. Indifference to values even while recording them is one of the greatest destroyers of values there is because it attacks man's *very capacity to value*. This is why trifling art ultimately must be judged as being devoid of values and anti-value; for trifling art does not seek to give things value but deny their value, to deny *anything* having real value.

The trifling artists do not seek to elevate the human spirit because they themselves are not elevated in spirit. They present a view of life where nothing is held as meaningful, and this ideal can be dumped out only from a soul which holds life itself as being essentially meaningless.

The trifling artist does not speak like a God should, in the most elevated tone about the most elevated of things; he speaks as if there is nothing divine about man, as if there is nothing divine at all!

The trifling artist will denounce the ideal of being idealistic in art, his objection expressed in their stock answer, 'this is not the way most people are'. His objection based on the fact idealism presents what man can be and not what he generally is. He further qualifies his objection by saying that the idealist is an escapist and not a realist like him. The answer to that is the way things are is exactly why we need art, to show us the way life should be so we will change life from what it is into what it should be. Exalting idealism *is* escapism, the key that opens the door allowing escape from a lower to a higher way of life. The realist is willing to be imprisoned in the dreary reality his realism demands he accepts.

My opposition to trifling is not primarily aesthetic, (though there are reasons enough in this area to oppose it), my opposition is moral, for art's purpose is to lead man to something higher and trifling art essentially leads man nowhere.

Worse even than to take your readers nowhere is to take them crawling down through the sewers to wallow in depravity. Here we arrive at the polar opposite of us idealist, the other school of (twisted) thought on what should be the spirit of writing, which is what I call the depravity school of writing, or the sewer writers. The depravity writers depict man as he should not be, man at his most depraved and worst. The depravity writers do not merely depict human evil and depravity, they *glorify it*. The depravity writers *revel* in depicting the worst in humans and in showing life at its worst. From the depraved writer's pages flow forth the humanly worst: killers, gangsters, the insane, the useless, violence, disease, tragedy, despair, angst, hopelessness, suffering, death. In the presentation of their rogue's galleries of losers and psychos and their many evil and worthless ideals as they stand for what man should not be they stand against what man should be.

A variation on the depravity school is those who show not man but *reality* as being depraved and horrible. The goal of this school is to project a sense of reality that shows the world is inherently depraved and brutal, that man is in the control of malevolent forces that will make his life a living hell. In this case the depravity writer's depict not man as evil but reality as evil and man as helpless before it.

In the one case the goal is to show that the nature of man is bad, in the other that the nature of reality is bad and man helpless before it; in both cases they show human life as being a living hell. They show man as a devil or being tormented eternally by devils. The depraved writer's ultimate goal is to project a view of life to the reader that life is not worth living, and I label him as being depraved because what is truly depraved about him is his ultimate message.

Depraved art is a malevolent light shining upon the worst and allowing men to see only that, a light which seeks to leave the good shrouded in darkness.

The depraved writer renounces his chance to be a God and opts instead to be a devil, a destroyer of the values of this world and the concept of the value of this world. To open up a depraved work is to turn the key which opens up the pit of hell.

The depraved artist takes his readers on journeys thru hell and lingers on the agonies of the damned. The idealistic writer does not take such journeys, does not spend his time gawking at the damned; taking a journey to see the joys of the blessed, yes.

The depraved writer unleashes inky defecations upon the page and calls this literary crap art, the foul odor of such art disgusting and turning off the human spirit. The depraved artist call their crap art using the title art as bait to lure in the unsuspecting unaware of what they are being hooked by, and once hooked they end up breathing in the depraved spirit that holds the line. The spirit of a depraved art works to bring down any exposed to it, by breathing in such foul literary airs it makes the reader's spirit feel despair, disgust, angst, hopelessness, hatred, i.e. it makes him less willing or even unwilling to live life.

In the depravity school they are using words to denounce and damn human existence, thru the stand against values, thru the sneering at all human aspiration for values, thru the open lust for the destruction of values, showing man as being devoid of value, thru using art as the means to say no to the value of human life.

Here is the ultimate truth and cause of the depravity school— with the depraved artists the root cause of their depravity is they hate humans and human life. The artist's work is always the testament of his soul. If an artist creates a book which is anti-life then he is anti-life. Depraved art is the whip the life-haters use to strike at life. Their dark twisted writing becomes a reflection of the true nature of their soul, a soul turned dark and twisted. The truth of the twisted darkness of their souls is found in reading a depraved literary work, the spirit of such books clearly the airing of a soul which does not want to be alive. The depraved writer having lost his will to live seeks from life only to take the will to live of others.

The depravity school glorifies evil though as a means to an end; those who raise up evil do so in order to bring down the good. To make a stand for evil is to stand against the good; to raise up the lowest most botched form of human being is to seek to stamp down the highest human possible. With those who create depraved art they do not want human greatness to exist, they do not want to see man raised to his rightful place, they do not want to see man elevated and exalted. The depravity writers aim their words at the human spirit to hit it and bring it down; the human spirit once brought down this ensures they will never have to see their greatest horror realized, man raised up to the point of greatness.

Why cut the wings off the human spirit and bring it down? The depraved in spirit denounce the good and great within man because they themselves lack it, and they do not want to see it realized within other men. The depraved human beings resent the good because the good represent what they betrayed. The good reflect back to the depraved what they truly are, and the bad wish to smash that mirror so they do not have to see such a horrible reflection. The depraved artists present human depravity in their works not because human depravity exists but because it exists within them; they want human depravity to flourish because it rationalizes to them their own spiritual depravity.

The depraved artists who ink such works when attacked for presenting books with such an awful spirit often try to defend their works by taking a realist stance, saying my pen merely records the way humans are. Their stance collapses before the fact that the majority of men are good yet they never record this. The truth is those who pose as recorders of depravity do so in order to hide their own depravity. To point the finger at the bad minority while never pointing once to the majority who are good is to finger oneself as being a bad person. The real reason depraved artworks are created is because they are a vent for the spirit of the one writing them.

The pen always records the nature of the soul wielding it. In the end all writers leave an imprint of their soul on their pages. Writers when talking of anything are always talking of themselves. Writing is or should be only for a soul that has something worthwhile to say. Writing is a soul leaving an enduring expression of itself on the written page. When the soul is noble writing becomes one of the highest forms of self-expression. The problem with writing recording the nature of the soul is that some souls are so ugly that it is better if no page ever recorded their imprint.

The idealist artist records people who are passionate valuers, passionately pursuing their values, created by a person who is a passionate valuer. The trifling artist shows people of little importance maybe pursuing values but values of little importance, created by a person who values little if at all and if he values values only little things. The depraved artist shows people passionately dedicated to the destruction of values, created by a person who shares their passion for destruction.

When reading an idealistic artist work I know you burn with a love of life; with the trifling artist I know your fire of life has burned out or was never lit; with the depraved artist I know you burn with a hatred against life.

Those who glorify evil or define how to be it in their non-fiction works are showing us the true nature of their own souls. The good do not glorify evil or write how to books to help cultivate it.

You should not stick your nose into a book that delves into and revels in the worst of humans and human life for the same reason you should not stick your nose in a sewer. Nor should you create artistic sewers. Value yourself enough as an artist and as a human being to raise yourself above the level of creating what belongs in a sewer.

Do not glorify depravity, cruelty, human wickedness, i.e. evil within your works; do not lower yourself by glorifying the lowest of humans; do not write fiction works that highlight serial killers, gangsters, dictators, showing the evil in action; do not write non-fiction works which explain how to rob, terrorize, murder, how to put evil in action; do not show the worse in humans or appeal to or encourage the worst in humans in your works; do not dedicate your life's work to the destruction of life.

My opposition to the depraved spirit in art comes from the fact that my spirit is not depraved, a fight fought not just on artistic grounds but on moral grounds, mine fought for man as the best he can be and the depraved fought to ensure man at his best cannot be.

It is artistically unappealing and morally wrong to put the primary focus of an artwork on the weird, freaky, sick and wicked; not when there is so much good in man and men to focus on.

Does the exalting ideal say that there should be no depictions of flawed or evil humans or inhuman ideals within literary works? No! *Negatives can be included but only as a way to highlight the positive.* Evil humans and the dark motives that move them can be included within a work but *only* as a means to *highlight* their opposite, the good humans and the ideals that move them and make them the good. The darkness can be used as a means to frame the light. Evil, corruption and the darkness that can sometimes be in man should be used in art only as a means to further highlight the good, noble and virtuous that is more likely to be in man. Immoral people can be used to teach moral lessons. In art the bad must always serve as a means to the good.

This is also true of depicting insignificant people, for their depiction can be used to highlight the significant people. Small people work to make the large people seem larger than life.

The depiction of human evil and/or human insignificance within a idealistic work is not something that stands in contradiction to the purpose of idealism, of showing ideal humans, for their depiction is not an end but a means to an end, the evil or insignificant serving as the frame upon which the good can stand up and be clearly shown for what they truly are.

The proper purpose for the depiction of the insignificant and evil is to use them as a means to highlight the good, to clarify further the meaning of the good, to serve as a foil for the good and/or give the good something to triumph over.

In showing a struggle between good and evil this does not mean it should be sugarcoated, the equivalent of an after school special; the goal in fiction of showing such struggles is to increase the suspense and drama of the struggle as much as possible and what must be shown in the end is the clear *triumph* of the good.

In a fictional work the hero's virtuous nature should never be in doubt, and undoubtedly and completely virtuous yet the story if well done should make you doubt whether the virtuous will triumph until the end when the virtuous hero triumphs beyond all doubt.

A depraved writer depicts evil men in order to damn man as such. An idealistic writer depicts evil men in order to damn only evil men. (Moreover, this denouncement is a secondary goal aiding in the primary goal of glorifying the good men.) The trifling artist does not make any kind of stand for or against man.

There is in the idealistic realm of art a proper and moral place for the focused study of evil, but not because the evil are worthy of study in and of themselves but because the good are worthy of being fought for which sometimes requires a study of the nature of evil. Intentions can perform moral alchemy; the end desired making what is normally a moral wrong morally right. In a case where the artist makes it his primary goal to depict evil in order to denounce it because of worthy intentions this makes it an example not of depravity but of nobility, for the goal is worthy, to protect and cultivate the good man and the good life, but doing so in a negative way, by exposing the nature of evil showing the means to deal with that evil thus protecting the good from that evil. There is a potential problem though in writing a book where the writer's intent is primarily focused on evil, where evil becomes the *only* focus of such a book. Here we come to the denunciatory artist, those who show only negatives, who depict evil and only evil and only as a means to denounce or stop evil yet are unable or unwilling to depict the good; here the denunciatory artist makes us enter an arena where nothing but evil exists; here is an arena the human spirit can endure only for so long and only so long as it remembers the good worth fighting for, something the denunciatory artist fails to provide. When contemplating a denunciatory work of art while I find myself approving of the goal of such works, to denounce and stop that which is wrong or evil in this world, I find that with artworks where the focus is solely on evil even if in order to denounce the evil even though their intentions were good the works in spirit feel depraved. These kinds do not revel in the fact that sewers exist, yet they focus only on such things. Even though we both agree that sewers are unpleasant this is all such works still smell of. They do not glorify evil, seeking with sincerity to bring it down, yet fail in their works to glorify the good, and so focused upon bringing evil down cannot uplift the good.

Those who are against evil yet focus on it in their writings are perhaps ascribing to a belief of evil as being more powerful than the good, a power which it does not possess. Evil is irrationality, evil is impotence, the evil represent the self-defeated. The corrupt and evil are always doomed to defeat not necessarily by the nature of the good who struggle against them but ultimately by the very nature of their own twisted natures. In the world of art the evil should be shown as they are in the real world, doomed to defeat by their very own irrationality. Evil in a literary work should be laughed at or despised but never glorified or elevated in stature over the good. From here on I banish the hateful and indifferent to human values from any artistic and *human* consideration leaving room only for the idealist, the highest value in art because he is the highest valuer of humans and human life.

Idealism the only worthy literary standard

The ideal or spirit of writing that I am stating should be the goal of all writers I call idealism—idealism in that it presents man at his best, and it does so by appealing to the best that is within man; its sum will exalt man in art and in reality exalt man in spirit, and this is the highest goal art can add up to.

There is always an exhilarating thrill that runs through me whenever I enter the world of an idealistic spirit, and I lose myself in his or her world. I can remember reading the idealistic works, of heroes and their epic quests, a world of adventure, romance, virtue, heroism, where men acted as men should. I look for and read only books with such an idealistic spirit for such a spirit matches my own. When I go to a book I say to it uplift me to heaven. I do not say to any book try and drag me into the sewer; if any book makes the attempt it is itself flushed into the sewer. I do not say to a book bore me with the insignificant, and if I come across such a book I take it for what it is, a book of no real significance, and give it no more of my significant time. I want to read only books by someone who actually is happy to be alive and sung it out in their art; I read such books because the feeling of being happy to be alive is the kind of feeling I want from books, what I want from *anything*.

Idealistic art transforms you; you are one person when you begin reading them, another when done. Idealistic works are the kind you buy and read and reread and even carry physically around with you, and more so such books you always carry around within you spiritually. You read these exalted works again and again, reading as a means to spark the mind, to stoke the spirit, to kindle happiness. The kinds of books which posses a idealistic spirit are a true treasure to have, a joy to read in and of themselves, a joy to apply to your life, a joy that you continue to carry around with you after you are done reading and their spirit lingers on within you.

If the goal of the idealist artist is to create the most heroic life-affirming art the world has ever seen this goal when achieved has the greatest power to transform the world for the good and for the greatest good.

Only the idealistic spirit and purpose in art can fulfill the moral goal of art, to uplift the human spirit. All other forms of art by their very nature will fail to fulfill the moral goal of art, for they either cannot move the spirit or move it in the right direction. Denunciatory art which stands against evil yet fails to show the good fulfills a moral goal for art but not *the* moral goal of art, it protects the human spirit from being lowered yet it cannot uplift it. Trifling writing only boring the human spirit cannot move it, it can achieve no moral goal. Depravity writing depressing the human spirit only lowers it, its goal is immoral.

Approach your work with a belief in human greatness and in time that belief will be shining back to you from the pages and you will have produced a work of *human* greatness.

Besides the end goal of producing a book actually worth reading the principle of exalting idealism offers two more personal benefits— writing as an idealist benefits you both as a writer and as a human being. Being an idealistic writer benefits you as a writer by 1—making the writing process a pure joy because as you are creating a world worth living in your writing you lose yourself in that joyful benevolent world as you are creating it. It is a true joy to lose yourself in an ideal world even if it only exists on paper, and 2—creating idealistic art also benefits the writer as a human being by making him into a better human being. In the exploration of ideas the writer defines not just for his work what ideas it will hold but what ideas he will hold. Writing is often the art of self-exploration and self-creation. As you create your art you also are in effect creating yourself. To make explicit what had before been implicit, to follow old ideas to shocking new conclusions, to reform ideas, to add to them, to subtract, performing moral mathematics, learning what you are, what you should be, what you need to do to remake yourself into what you should be. An artistic discipline often becomes a spiritual one.

Writing takes what is spiritually immaterial and makes it a concrete reality. As religions carve their ideals into stone so too should you do the equivalent, for ideals carved into stone makes the ideas clear and concrete, ideals you can now hold and live by.

By setting your sights so high in your writing you then take that idealistic spirit and use it to soar to your own peak in life. The idealistic spirit is the wings which will uplift you to the peak of what life can be.

Set your artistic standards to the highest humanly possible—here is the only standard worth following in anything you do. Do not set your standards to the average or the lowest humanly possible; do not turn down or off your potential, for greatness lies within you. Setting your moral standard to the highest possible is the key which unleashes your potential in the form of greatness. To be a great writer do not set your standard to a depraved one which causes you to show the worst humans and the worst human life can be, and making you into the worst kind of artist and person you can be. Do not allow your artistic standard to be set at mediocrity, making for mediocre art and making you a mediocrity. Set your standard to the highest possible which shows only the best in man and life, the idealistic standard, and which will raise your art and yourself up to greatness. Write to show not everyday life or the worst in life but to show the high values that matter in life and which elevate life to the best it can be. This is the only kinds of works I want to write and read. I hope that by now you do to.

In closing this essay my exalting banner is now raised high and flying clearly. In this essay I have served as the herald of the ideals that elevate the literary art into a religion—art is a means to glorify and sanctify human life. By the ideals set forth in this essay I raise art above mere entertainment, above pastime, above a career, and raise it to the level of a holy crusade.

Let the ideals set forth in this essay be your reasons why you write; let the banner of exalted idealism be your artistic banner. Become a crusader for and a creator of idealistic art; assume the divine mission to raise man to his proper place in this world. The ideals of idealism once they become yours raise you to your proper place in this world, for they give value to your writings, give value to your writing life, make you into a better writer and a better human being, will create a passion for the writing process and above all else give you a passion for life itself.

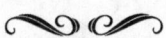

Part three—
What Should I write?

4

The Art of Choosing Form

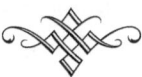

Choosing the form your art will take is an art in itself. A great idea can get perverted or even lost in the wrong artistic form. The great idea needs the right form to carry it.

The proper moral purpose of writing is to capture and present the ideas that matter in human living—this is why you should write, this is the ultimate goal to aim for, yet such an ideal does not tell you what is the best form for presenting your ideas.

There are many forms of writing, all very capable of carrying ideas—novels, short stories, plays, poetry, song lyrics, essays, manuals, speeches, fables, comics, editorials, movies to name but a few forms.

Writers over the centuries have invented many forms of writing. Many more forms will be invented. New ideas will need new forms.

The purpose of writing is to carry ideas to the mind. Therefore the proper way to choose the form you will write in is this, look at the idea you wish to present and then decide on the best form for carrying it.

The literary art has to carry many different ideas to the mind; the purpose of differing literary forms is having different vehicles for carrying different ideas.

The form of writing is the vehicle for carrying an idea. Every form of writing has inherent advantages and disadvantages. You would not use a compact car to carry furniture, nor use a tractor trailer to pick up groceries. So too should you not use a long novel to carry a simple idea, nor use a short story to tell a complex philosophy.

In writing you should not approach it with a set form in mind and you will try and fit your ideas into that form but approach it with your ideas set and you will employ the form which will best fit your ideas. A man built like a sumo wrestler should not be put on a basketball court because he cannot move very well, nor should a tall thin man be put in the sumo ring, for he cannot withstand the weighty clash. Ideas like men stand their own way, some are lofty, some weighty, some need a heavy serious format to be carried in, others need a lofty one.

For example in deciding how to present your ideas on the subject of freedom weighty philosophical essays may be the best form if you wish to define its philosophical meaning or if you want to show the exact meaning and consequences of its lacking and the real meaning of why people desire freedom it may be best to present it in a work of lofty fiction of people suffering under and rebelling against a state of tyranny for here rather than talking in the abstract about it you put its essence and meaning in human form. Which form you choose depends on what exactly you wish to say about the idea of freedom.

In determining what form to write in the three things that should be considered is 1—what is the idea I want to present 2—what is it that I want to say about that idea and 3—what is the best means of projecting the idea? First define the idea you want to project and only then determine the best means to project it.

Most writers though do things in reverse. For example they decide to write an action adventure story and then begin a plot and maybe try to add in some idea of moral value to make the story worth reading. Oftentimes what detracts from the value of the works is that the moral ideas are secondary to the action element, the projecting of action assumes primacy over the projection of ideas, and so the book written gets slanted in the wrong direction, that which matters the most, the ideas, gets focused on the least, and often the action form may not even be the best way to project those particular ideas. Many writers become more committed to a particular literary form than to the ultimate purpose of literary forms, *ideas*. An adventure story filled with action yet devoid of high ideas and meaning would not be worth reading no matter how well done the action sequences are. Today often in books and even more often in movies we see action works which are almost nothing but action with little to no moral meaning attached to them, and all of these works artistically are failures. Such is the nature and consequences of men who approach their works without the right ultimate goal, to project meaningful ideas, and only then choosing the best means to project those ideas.

In creating an action work with a hero you should not use the hero to show action but use action in order to show a hero. (The true meaning of a hero.)

Characters are really for carrying ideas, the ideas of what a hero is, a villain is etc. A character without an idea to carry is someone who carries no weight in the work.

For most writers they often have an affinity or liking for a particular form or they are just naturally better at projecting their ideas in that form. Oftentimes a writer predetermines the form in which he wants to project ideas because the way his mind works naturally suits it to that particular form of writing. This attitude of sticking to one literary form can be artistically limiting, but so long as the writer does not lose sight of the primary goal of writing, the projection of ideas, he can write works worth reading.

Sometimes a writer decides I am only going to write action stories, or essays, or poetry, and this attitude while limiting and cutting him off from much that writing has to offer to him he in having this attitude can still produce superior literary works *if* he approaches his writing with the attitude that my *ultimate* goal is not to write essays or action stories but to project the ideas that matter in human living, only I am going to limit myself to doing it thru this one literary form.

The writer who writes in his times

Many artist create within the accepted practices of their times. They create according to popularly accepted forms without ever really questioning those forms deeply. There is nothing necessarily morally wrong with this, especially if the artist in following the times is in an enlightened time and the times fit his ideas. An artist though may find his ideas too great for the style of the times. An artist if he is dedicated to following the times has to end up following the times for better or for worse; and if worse his dedication to the times *limits his greatness*. This is where following the path of tradition takes a turn for the worse. An artist who breaks free of the times follows his own path, whether well worn or a completely new one, his path always turns for the better, never for the worse.

Many artist (and people) let the times define them rather than define their time for themselves.

Many artists (and people in general) allow themselves to be bound by tradition. Here are men bound not by their time but a time long dead. A time that may have no relevance to the living present. So many allow themselves to be guided by the dead hand of tradition, guided by a corpse no longer alive to the changing times. The fact that other men once thought so does not we must think as they did *especially* if we can *think better* than they did. Tradition bounds men to a past that may not be as wise as the present. Men in their times created as best they could by the *limited* knowledge they held at that time. As time and knowledge advance so to must we. When we bound ourselves to the past we bound ourselves not just to what the past knew but to all the past *did not know*. If we are able to see better than those of the limited past we with this greater sight can move on to greater things *if* we do not bound ourselves to the blindness of the past.

Knowledge cannot advance when bound in tradition's chains. For if men want to be advancing in knowledge so too must the ignorance caught by tradition be jettisoned for a better wiser present. As times change so too must men to meet them; better yet is men changing the times to suit themselves.

The only relevant question is not how did men do it in the past but what is the best way to do it. (And to answer this we can learn from the past but cannot be limited by it.)

The idea of breaking from tradition is breaking from things as they are to things as they *should be.* If no one had broken from the times we would all still be living in caves. When the times are no longer great enough for a man he must break from those times to achieve a better way of doing things; it is this breaking from the times that is the source of all human progress.

Contrast—The use of positive and negative forms

There are two ways to project ideas, through positive or negative illumination. We can show or explain the meaning of an idea through showing a positive application of it, or we can illustrate it in a negative way by showing what happens when it is absent. For example in showing the need for courage we can show why men need to be courageous in a fiction story by showing a courageous man and exactly what consequences his courage brings to him. We can also show the need for courage by showing what happens when it is lacking, showing the coward in action (or inaction) and what consequences his cowardice bring unto him. Generally speaking the best way to project an idea whether in fiction or non-fiction is through showing both the positive and negative meaning of it *together.* For example if you wish to write a novel showing the importance of being courageous besides showing courageous men in action and the kinds of consequences they reap from their courage to fully illustrate your meaning you should also display besides them the cowardly characters and the kind of lives their cowardly nature reaps for them. When we show an idea in a purely positive light, for example in a story showing only men of courage, it says this is what men of courage do and what happens to them because of their courage, yet it leaves unanswered what are the consequences of cowardice? How are men to be drawn to being courageous when they have not been given a reason to be drawn from being cowards? The same thing happens when we do things in reverse, if we show or tell about only the cowards it does not tell men the benefits of being a courageous man. How are men going to grasp and hold onto a virtue if they have not grasped the benefits of holding it? To show the full meaning of the right way we must show the nature of both the right and the wrong ways. Oftentimes the full meaning of an idea only gets understood only when its opposite or when its lacking is seen. This is why oftentimes the best way to truly show or tell about some idea is to show it in both a positive and negative illumination. Here I present the idea of contrast into art, of showing the two sides of everything. Here the two extremes each become a light to help illuminate the other extreme. To use a dark frame to display a bright picture makes the picture stand out even brighter yet. Try to use contrast to make the light of your ideas shine even brighter from the page.

Fiction and non-fiction

All forms of writing basically fall into two categories, fiction and non-fiction, story and theory, to show or to tell.

In non-fiction its essential purpose is to explain the meaning of an idea. In fiction its essential purpose is to show the meaning of an idea in action.

In non-fiction the goal is to explain or define the exact meaning of an idea; the ultimate goal is thru explanation to make the reader understand in and give him the means whereby they can apply the idea to their own lives.

The purpose of fiction is to show an idea in action. Fiction writing is through a story using the character and events in the story to show the meaning and application of some idea as embodied in men actually acting on or for that idea. (Or even the consequences to men who fail to act on or for that idea.) We see the idea in action and are inspired to take action on it.

In the two forms of writing, fiction and non-fiction, there is a great power in each, and each has its own way of getting ideas across, and we should use these differing forms of literary power as appropriate to get our ideas across.

In non-fiction is the abstract theory, in fiction is the theory put into concrete action. In idealism non-fiction we are often defining how to become ideal men living the ideal lives; the goal is to give us the theory behind the ideal. In idealism fiction the goal is to show the ideal men in action, to be shown for inspiration as well as emulation. In fiction we see the consequences of an idea put into action and are inspired to take action on it. Men can look at the fictional ideal and say yes that is worth working for. Inspired by the fiction works readers can then refer back to the theoretical works and can use them to figure out how to become those ideal men living the ideal lives.

There is something very inspiring about fiction writing. A writer is creating his own world, history, life itself, he is like a God in that while within this reality of the fiction work as he wills it so it is. Yet non-fiction writing is also equally a divine act. There is something very spiritual about intellectually writing your way to the basic essence and meaning of a great idea. The writer captures for all eternity an idea. In non-fiction the writer can sculpt ideas into tablets to serve as commandments for men. Both forms, fiction and non-fiction, when done under the right premises and in the right way, are equally valid, and can be of equal benefit to human living. You should never close your mind to either form, but in deciding how to project your ideas use the form which is best suited to projecting your ideas.

Many writers may decide I do not want to write non-fiction because I do not want to write dry, boring discussions. Some may decide I do not want to do fiction because I want to write serious stuff, not silly stories. In this case it is not the nature of non-fiction or fiction writing that is unsuited to them it is their attitudes to those forms which is unsuited to being a writer. Non-fiction when done under the right premises is anything but dry or boring. Read the so called dry works of the great minds of non-fiction, they are alive and burning and challenging and rewarding. Fiction works when also done under the right premises is not just silly stories, it is a chance to show in the action of a story the highest possible to man.

Reaping the whole field of writing

A great danger to you as an artist is to indulge snobby elitism, where you cut yourself off from whole fields of writing. Snobby elitism does not raise your standards but places a fence around them that your standards cannot expand beyond. The barrier of snobbishness does not really place unworthy things beneath you but cuts you off from many great and worthy things by placing them out of your reach. For example many see poetry as effeminate, cutting themselves off from the beauty of the poetic fields. Many look down on graphic novels as 'being for kids', ignoring the combination of literature and drawing can give a far greater depth to an artwork.

Many writers suffer from form limitation attitude. They reject outright the writing in a particular form. They let their artistic and personal limitations determine the form. This attitude limits all the possibilities open for their work in that style. Rejecting outright a form of writing is rejecting a potential challenge, a great achievement and a new joy. Rejecting outright a literary form is rejecting what will be the best vehicle for carrying certain ideas. The idea is what should determine the form. It is the idea that matters more than the form, as the building is of greater importance than the tools used to build it.

The important thing about becoming a good artist (or becoming good at anything) is to not place limitations upon yourself. Drop all your self-imposed limitations and let your genius expand to its true dimensions.

The artist limited by his times or artistic conventions limits his genius. Genius should *never* have limits placed upon it.

The goal of this essay is to open up your mind to all forms and types of writing, so you may not be limited by an attitude, so your genius may have an open horizon before it. Let your genius go wherever it needs to and let no snobbery or attitude ever stop it or even limit it. Since all literary forms can be used for presenting ideas, and one form may be better in some cases than the other, the goal is to keep an open mind and to allow the nature of the idea to dictate the form to be used. My advice to writers is to not close your mind to any form, and to work in all forms, using the special attributes of each form to your advantage. I myself work in many differing forms and have found that each form presents me with special challenges, and each gives its own special rewards.

As variety is the spice of life so it is in writing to. A writer could burn out writing only one way. Writing in different forms, projecting values in different ways, this variety adds up to making a writing career far more challenging and interesting.

Writing in one form also makes you a better writer in the other forms. For example in writing poetry this gives you a better sense of rhythm and timing, which can be used even in writing technical essays.

The goal in this essay was not to fence anyone towards any particular form of writing but to tear down the fences and open the whole literary field of artistic forms to being harvested. The goal is to help the artist determine what is the best form to write in by giving to the artist the right perspective to judge from. Do not lose sight of the goal of projecting your ideas; use this as your sole means to determine what form you will write in. The goal desired will often tell you the best means to achieve it. The field of writing is an immense field with many types of fruits that can be harvested from it, a veritable Garden of Eden, and the wise writer who has learned the art of choosing form opens up the whole literary garden to being harvested.

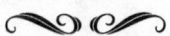

Part four—
How Should I write?

5

Word-Painting—
Painting Pictures with Words

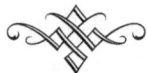

Style is the carriage upon which ideas are carried to the reader. A great stylist moves us thru his style of using words, moving us into his literary world. Yet more than that a great style can become the carriage that emotionally moves us. The great question of style is what is the method that allows words to move people?

Many writers have little grasp of the principles and purpose of style and so spend most of their time groping around in the dark for the right words. Even writers who have something of a philosophy on writing often find themselves stumbling around in a twilight world marked with only occasional glimpses of light. By holding a clear philosophy on writing in knowing your goal and the methods that will lead you to it this knowledge creates the light by which you can always see the path.

Many writers have no method to their style, are not even aware you need a method. The methodless writer when he knows what he wants to write about now the question of how, the question of style, arises before him, and he has no answer to it. They who do not understand the style of using words just throw words onto the page hoping a style will somehow emerge from their random throwing, and once the words are on the page have no idea how to shape what they blindly grasped into a great style. Then there are the writers who have answered the question of style, they know where to go to grasp words and how to shape them on the written page.

The writer who grasps the goal of style but not its methods will end up drawing pictures in the dark. The writer who fails to understand the goal and purpose of style is not writing but just scribbling.

Excellence in style, as with excellence in anything, will emerge consistently only when you fully grasp its ultimate purpose—*the purpose of style is to carry the meaning of an idea to the mind. Style is the transporter of ideas.*

Style is form, not content or idea. In writing form follows content, style follows the idea. Style carries the idea. Style is the servant of ideas. Idea is the meaning of each sentence, what you want the parts (words) to add up to, and style serves the idea by carrying its meaning to the mind.

Writing is the art of making thought visible. Words give shape to thoughts. Be it a person, a place, an event, a feeling, or an abstraction the writer is using words to give shape to the idea that is in his head.

For the purpose of transporting ideas not all styles are created equal. An illustrative style carries ideas clearly to the mind. A muddy style tends to lose ideas in transit. The non-visual style kills the meaning of an idea in its place.

The purpose of style being to carry ideas then the goal in style is to use words in the ways where they become capable of carrying ideas.

The goal of style is to word-paint, using words to paint literary pictures which illustrate the idea. Word-painting is where the way words are used causes visual images to form of the idea, the mind now can see the idea and able to picture it can understand it.

Style is the means by which the writer embodies the spiritual realm of ideas. Style is the means by which the idea is given a living form. A good style brings the idea to life. The goal in seeing this living idea is in viewing its form its meaning may be seen by the mind.

Word-painting is the term I use to describe an illustrative style of writing. In the dictionary the term illustrative means several things 1—to make clear, 2—to enlighten, 3—to provide with visual features intended to explain or decorate, and 4—to make illustrious. These definitions all define the illustrative word-painting style. The goal of all writing is to clearly articulate the meaning of ideas, for the purpose of enlightening the mind, doing so by using words in such a way that they draw up visual images of the meaning of the idea being discussed, and the words both make the idea illustrious and the manner in which the words are arranged make themselves illustrious.

The word-painting style reverses the religious formula, the flesh is made word; for the reader this process reverses itself, things take their spiritual flesh in their minds from the words.

The motto of the great stylist—I will create the world, give light to it, color it in glorious tones, make life flower all thru it. The word-painter often sees himself as a God before his own Eden which he must fill in with form and color and life.

The standouts in the field of writing always used a visual form of writing. Their writing moved you to enlightenment, they shined the light of their minds on an idea and you saw what they wanted you to see.

Why word painting works—we think in images. For example when I say the word warrior do you think in terms of words or images? Do you think a man who professionally fights to protect a society? No! You may think of or see the image of a heavily muscled Special Forces soldier, in camouflage, face painted black, a large machine gun in his hand, or you more romantic types might see a white knight in shining armor. We do not really think in abstractions but in visual images of abstractions. (Which contain many words and ideas.) The word-painting style works because it conforms to man's way of thinking. Word-painting leads to an ah-ha reaction—when he says *this* he means *that*. As the ultimate goal of writing is to communicate the meaning of ideas word-painting serves this standard for it uses words in the way where we see the meaning and why it is meaningful to us.

There are two parts to writing, theme and style, or what it is you want to say and how do you want to say it. The principles of idealism in theme and word-painting in style are the principles that lead to great writing because they give to you the standards by which you can arrive at a proper theme and style for expressing it. In being an idealist who paints beautiful pictures with words you make both the destination and the journey to it worth the while. The initial goal of reading a work is to be transported into a beautiful literary fantasy world, and word-painting opens the door to this fantasy world for it allows the reader through the words he reads to draw up the right images and ideas in his mind; add the principle of idealism and this achieves the ultimate goal of writing, to not just transport the reader but transport him into a world *worth* living in.

The aspiration to the twin ideals of being a writer who is idealistic and word-paints flows from a mind which has an overflowing love of life guided by the supremacy of reason as the means to uphold that love—to hold the mind as the highest of human values, to express the highest values that can be conceived by the human mind, to express yourself in a manner best suited to the human mind, all for the purpose of serving human life, *this* is the justification for the ideal of being the word-painting idealistic writer. The commitment to these two ideals represents a commitment to rationality, or in other words a writer with a commitment to being a human being.

Presentation is almost as important as the ideas being presented. Great ideas can be easily lost to the mind by a style unworthy of the idea.

In poorly conceived books they fall short through a failure in intentions (goal). In poorly written works they fall short through a failure in execution (style).

The highest ideal of literary style—from words to make art and to make an art of words.

Since word-painting is a new term in writing there is a need to define its general ideals and methods which when followed will make an illustrative stylist. The word-painting style in regards to things is highly descriptive, it embodies the spiritual, uses visual imagery in the words themselves, in regards to abstractions it makes them concrete, it is heavily metaphorical, it paints things in a human context, it creates the proper spirit and has its own spirit, an effect is achieved through the spirit of the words and it always excites the human spirit.

Word-painting is descriptive—Word-painting describes in great detail persons, places and things. Word-painting is so descriptive of the literary world that it makes you see that world; it transports you to that world, you think you are there; or more accurately you can see yourself being there.

Word-painting causes pictures to form through its degree of being descriptive. For examples, the non-illustrative—He ate the apple. Word-painting—The golden haired child ate the shiny juicy red apple as he skipped through the lush green forest laughing with joy. The first case shows what happens when a writer fails to add color or even draw an outline of his idea, in reading it no clear picture emerges, the failure of style leaves us with no idea of what mood the person is in, where he is at, what the apple looks like, tastes like etc. The second case shows what happens when a master stylist paints with words, for images form, this colorful style takes us through a lush forest, we hear a laughing golden child, see a juicy red apple, and see the living spirit behind the actions.

The justification for descriptive word-painting lies in the fact that in writing we are writing about something in reality, an entity and its actions or spirit, so we have to draw up images of that thing and what it is doing or thinking or feeling. To describe reality we have to draw up images of reality.

Word-painting often relies upon fact layering, of using a mass of detailed facts to draw a clear picture. A mass of facts often drive your point home more clearly than telling people what you want them to think. Any rational man will reject the demands of another who tell him without proof what he should think. By painting pictures with words rather than telling people what to think the idea is to show people the facts that will show them what you want them to think about.

You define through details. To word-paint rather than giving an entity a generic label, a boy, an apple etc., you define the details of it that make that entity unique, a laughing golden haired boy, a shiny, juicy, red apple etc.

The great stylist defines. The poor stylist labels. Many writers label rather than define. For example a poor stylist will say the city was beautiful. Why you automatically ask? If the why remains unanswered, if the assertion remains unproven, the label given without proof holds no meaning to the mind. The word-painting stylist does not just say what something is but *why* it is. The illustrative writer would describe the beauty of the city by saying what is beautiful about it, the soaring towers, glowing lights, great arching bridges, colored cars swishing by etc. Word-painting in painting objective pictures becomes meaningful to the rational mind. Do not label, define. Do not give a generic label for an object; define the essence of an object.

Be precise in naming and describing things. Include details of reality in describing aspects of reality. Do not merely label. Labeling draws no clear picture in the mind, whereas defining the meaning of the label draws up an image to match the label. Do not say something is beautiful, for this could mean differing things for differing reasons; in saying something is beautiful say *why* it is so.

Describe concrete entities such as person, places, things in terms of their essential characteristics or natures, so the concrete entity being described does not emerge in thought as a fuzzy amalgamation of many similar entities but what is seen is a distinct unique entity in itself.

Sometimes to paint clear literary pictures you need to become literally descriptive—in describing an old man's face do not say his face looked old but his face looked like a totem pole wrapped in flannel. A totem pole in flannel creates a clear image while old can draw differing pictures.

Word-painting openly welcomes the liberal use of adjectives. Adjectives allow us to move from a generic label for an entity to show the details that make that entity unique. While the noun and verbs are always the most important part of a sentence since they represent subject and what it is doing adjectives are vital aids for word-painting for they add color to our pictures. In using a label noun no clear picture emerges or a picture emerges that is without color, just black and white; by adding in adjectives to it a clear single picture with color emerges.

Adjectives add the color to our pictures. Not just an apple but a shiny, red apple bursting with juice and flavor.

Verbs are very important for they put action into our pictures. Verbs are the energy in a sentence. They take the lifeless and bring it to life. Not just a kid moving but a kid skipping and laughing out loud for joy. Verbs are the difference between a still life and a *living* picture. Use strong active verbs. Verbs make your pictures move.

Engage the senses through your writing. Make the mind see more than a picture, make it smell a scent, hear a noise, feel a sensation, make it feel as if it is actually living in the scene. Such transportation heightens the awareness of the mind making it more willing to enter your literary fantasy world and to accept the values offered by that world.

Word-painting embodies the spiritual—Word-painting uses words to draw up visual images of concrete entities or the physical aspect of life; when we come to the other aspect of life, the spiritual, things reverse themselves and we often use visual images of concrete entities to describe what is going on in the spiritual world of man. For example when in the spiritual world and trying to describe the feeling of being emotionally trapped you can use the image of a prison to picture your meaning.

Word painting describes feelings and desires and emotions, or all that which is the spiritual aspect of life as if they are actual concrete entities.

In the spiritual world labels such as angry, happy etc. have little meaning, for they can have different meanings and vastly differing degrees in their meaning. Embodying or giving an image to a human emotion gives it an exact meaning and degree. For example you can describe hatred as a burning fire, or as an ice cold feeling, or as a sharp knife in one's side and by doing so embody the exact nature and degree of the feeling of that hatred.

Word painting uses visual imagery in the words themselves—Word-painting is not just using words to describe a visual image (a concrete entity) but when the words themselves become a visual image. This is using language as a visual medium, where language is no longer black words on a page but a living light showing you something. Word-painting uses visual imagery in the words themselves to describe something. Word-painting uses images such as iron curtain for tyranny, veils to represent secrecy, swords for justice etc.

Word-painting often uses symbolism, of imbuing an object with a deeper meaning. A sword in reality merely a weapon in the world of art under an artist skilled hands can become a symbol of freedom, or tyranny, of a hero or a villain, of good or evil.

Word-painting often uses images not just of entities but also of actions—running, cutting, soaring etc. Examples—Style is the carriage that moves us. Drawing pictures in the dark. Stumbling around in a twilight world.

Use figures of speech to draw up figures from speech.

Use such things as the dawn, the fall of night, the ocean waves waxing and waning, the rain falling, etc. as visual images to describe something in order to draw a deeper meaning.

Word-painting connects abstractions with concretes—Visual imagery is very much needed to describe the world of pure abstractions. The abstract is illustrated by defining it in terms as if it were an actual entity. Word-painting shows the concrete meaning or nature of an abstraction. Word-painting embodies the abstract. For example if you say it is evil this is non-illustrative as no picture emerges of exactly what evil is. In word-painting in trying to define the nature of evil if you picture evil as powerful you can paint it as being a large monster in chain mail armor, sword drawn to strike down the innocent. Or if you see it as being the petty and pathetic you can draw a picture of its nature as being like cockroaches, the many who are small, disgusting, pathetic, who scurry away at the sight of anything human. In each of these instances you by the nature of the words used draw a different picture of an abstract concept.

In expressing an abstraction in the mere labeling of the thing there can be a sense of disconnect from the reality of the thing. What this means is that the mind cannot picture the nature or meaning of the abstraction. By making an abstraction concrete it makes it real, an object with its own specific characteristics and nature.

With word-painting abstractions are tied to reality. In defining a concept the writer who has grasped the essence of the illustrative style does not use empty words that without the weight of meaning attached to them float away from this world, he makes the concept a real living aspect of this reality by tying the concepts meaning to reality through visual imagery.

In using abstractions such as statistics they can be detached from reality, from what our mind can picture, and so will often have no real meaning to the mind. Now word-painting would take a statistic and put it in a frame in which the mind can see its meaning. For an example if cancer kills twenty percent of the people in the world the non-illustrative stylist would simply quote this statistic, drawing an abstract picture, and his words will fail to move as no human being can picture what twenty percent of mankind looks like. Now in word-painting you would say "picture the five people you love most, odds are one of them standing in front of you is likely to die from cancer"; now any person can picture five people they love, an image is formed, the person now understands just how devastating cancer can be upon people and is moved by the picture formed. Word-painting puts the abstract in a light where a person can see its meaning.

Word-painting is often metaphorical—Now there are two forms of language, literal and metaphorical. Literal is calling it exactly as it is. Metaphorical is describing one thing through the terms normally used to describe something else. Metaphorical language is alternate reality wording, or mixing together two different worlds. For example saying her eyes were a blue sky, where the reader is given a clear cut picture of one concrete by comparing it to another concrete. Metaphors by marrying two different ideas together give birth to a new idea. The goal of metaphors is to use alternate wording to create fresh vivid images in a way that literal language cannot achieve.

The problem with literal language is it often fails to capture shades or degrees. Literal language gives the amalgamation, the general picture which draws upon many like entities. Metaphorical language works to capture the shades and degrees that literal language cannot capture that makes that entity unique.

Metaphors are vehicles you use to carry truth to the mind when truth cannot be seen directly.

Metaphors can do more than just draw pictures they can also project the deeper meaning of a subject in a way literal language often cannot. He led us tells us little about him as a leader, where he led like a lion shows not just a leader but a *strong* one. Not just that something happened (he led) but the full meaning of how he led (he led strongly).

Great writers thru metaphors capture not just the surface of something but the deep down essence of it. Literal language can often only scratch the surface whereas metaphorical language can often go to the core of a thing.

Metaphorical language should be used only in ways that deepen meaning. Metaphorical language is improperly used when it confuses or hides meaning, the metaphorical aspects of the sentence working to lead the mind astray from the pictures it should be arriving at. A literary sin—*the detached metaphor,* where the writer uses pretty sounding words that are not attached to any real meaning. The detached metaphor is a sin because the words seemingly something mean nothing. The sin is committed because the writer choose what looks good over what is good. A beautiful detached metaphor is like a beautiful woman without a mind, nice to look at perhaps but essentially useless.

Word-painting paints things in a human context—Word-painting often shows human actions and not just objects in action. Not the paper was thrown on the table but the man threw the paper on the table with a burning disgust. Humans have little interest in objects without such objects having a *human* meaning. The more important thing is not what is being done to an object but what a man is doing to the object and why he is doing it. For in art as in all things man is the most important of all things.

Show this world and people in a living active state. In saying something like the man threw the paper on the table rather than the paper was put on the table you are bringing life to the words by showing a living being in action rather than an object being thrown around. Bring the lifeless to life. Not active versus passive language but human versus nonhuman language, in which the human should triumph over the nonhuman.

Word-painting does not just describe places, people, events etc. but also shows the human spirit that is both cause and justification for what is happening. Spirit is not just what man did but why he did it, the thoughts and feelings which cause his actions. When we say the man threw the paper on the table with a burning disgust we show not just the man but the spirit (burning disgust) that caused his actions.

Word-painting creates the proper spirit towards the subject—Word-painting does more than paint pictures it paints them in a certain light. For example the word-painter in discussing the heroic does not just say it is heroic but uses heroic imagery which properly frames the concept making us see it in a heroic light.

The nature of the light shown on the subject sways the attitude in the direction appropriate towards the subject.

Word-painting does more than create intellectual knowledge, allowing us to see what the subject is, it also works to create our moral feelings upon the subject, the nature of the picture saying this is what we should think/feel about it.

The tonal light of our words represents not just what you are talking about but what should be our attitude towards it. Tone works to form a way of thinking towards the subject. A sarcastic tone works in one way, a serious tone in another.

Realize the *effect* you want to achieve with each paragraph, sentence and even word. Be aware even of punctuation. Does the idea you wish to convey require the spirit of being dramatic, ironic, sarcastic, defiant, heroic etc. Ideas have different natures and so do words as well. For example ripple is a word of bare significance, and should be used to describe people or events of bare significance. Now colossus is a word with weight behind it, and using it creates a heavy effect.

You do not just want to say mundanely a truth but strike the mind in the unique way you say it by illustrating the moral meaning and importance of the truth.

Be careful of having sentences with two tones or more. A symphony while it can have many variations must have one dominant theme. So too must a sentence and paragraph. Language must support and not stand against itself. Soft and silky go together, soft and brittle do not. No mixed metaphors for they draw up conflicting pictures. Two toned sentences represent words in conflict and are a literary sin because they create a battle for meaning in the mind.

Word-painting is illustrious and interesting in and of itself—This style of writing strives for the noble word, the colorful adjective, the grand noun, the active verb, words that embellish the pages, word structures that are unique and interesting to see in and of themselves, the pages bursting with pictures and ideas and life, the pages themselves coming to life, exciting to read and experience, the reader drawn to and moved by this literary life force.

Word-painting is not just painting pictures but painting them with flourish. Writers like painters can depict the same subject but can be interesting or boring depending on how they depict it. The illustrative stylist paints pictures bursting with color and action and spirit—with life itself!

The methods of word-painting—
How to wield the literary brush

First be clear on the picture—Once you have the idea you must then find a picture that will clearly illustrate your idea. To be able to paint clear literary pictures first you must be clear on the picture you wish to draw and only then will you be able to choose the words capable of drawing such a picture. If you have not come to an image the words will not arrive to draw it. How can you draw pictures with words if you have no clear idea of the exact picture you wish to draw?

When writing you must not try to see words but to see what it is you are trying to describe, see the object, person, place etc. and the words to describe it will follow. Not just a person but what kind of person, a vile repulsive villain in a black cape, a young warrior in shining armor, a golden haired maiden etc.

Find a picture to frame your idea in. When you know the idea you want to describe then find the image that will best show what it means. For example in talking about the forming of character you could use the image of a sculpture to describe how character is formed and use sculpting imagery and metaphors throughout the work.

Know thy image and the words for it will follow.

Many writers start with a blank sheet and a blank mind; they begin writing without being able to picture what they want their writing to become, just splashing literary paint onto the page hoping that their jumble of words will *somehow* add up to a worthy picture. In the end they usually end up drawing an abstract picture, one with no meaning. Or the picture that emerges is so muddy the picture is hard to understand and unappealing to view.

A blank page should not be pulled out until the mind is filled with worthy ideas and images to fill it with. When you see the idea and the image to define it they will tell you which words they should be drawn in. Find an image that shows your idea.

Audition words—See yourself when writing as a casting director for words. Try different words in the sentence and see which performs better in the role. Remember the words must serve the idea, so try different words to see which serves it better. Each word like each person has a different nature, making them perfectly suited for some roles, perfectly unsuited for others. Words have color, form, personalities, a particular nature, and each word added or subtracted will redraw the picture. To change one word can dramatically redraw the whole literary picture. Do not rush the audition; audition words until each role is filled by the right word.

The principle for choosing words—choose words that can do the work to move an idea; not just words that can move an idea but words that move an idea and move the reader in doing so. Words must touch the mind before they can imprint themselves in it.

Strive for clarity, i.e. crystal clear writing—Word-painting is achieved through clarity, clear precise expression that once read is instantly understood without any doubts. Clarity is writing in terms that are *clear to the understanding of any rational mind.* Clarity is achieved when in describing any event, person, concept etc. by using the fewest clearest words that best illuminate your meaning.

When your pen is guided by the ideal of clarity this ensures that the writing is not dull and blunt, that it is made clear and sharp. The sharper your point the deeper it will penetrate into the mind of your reader.

In writing with clarity your goal is not to meet popular standards or even certain artistic standards but to meet a *human* standard. The goal of clarity is to make a statement of pure rationality. The goal in employing clarity is to act not as if you are addressing a mob but are addressing a human mind.

Writing is the art of communication. As far as rules of grammar, style, spelling is concerned all that which aids in clear communication is the good and all that which inhibits clear communication is the bad.

To give clarity to a paragraph is to give it an exact meaning, and exactness is the hallmark of the ideal writer, the objective writer. The ideal of the objective writer—each paragraph should be written in a way that ensures it has only one meaning. With many writers their flaw is to employ words in a way where their words can have different meanings, or worse yet no meaning. Many when referring to these types of works call them rich, or complex, meaning they can have many different meanings, or their meaning is not easily understood. Words like complex in being used to describe a work are usually a sign of failure in the work, for complexity is a word that states clearly that the work is not drawing clear pictures for the reader.

Clarity is also a result of moral courage, of not being afraid to say exactly what you mean. In the way you write make your stand, leave no doubts about it and make no apologies for it.

Simplify—The principle of simplicity—to cut away all that is unnecessary. The ideal of simplicity—to try to say as much as you can with as few words as you can. Or in other words speak little but say much. Simplicity does not mean cutting ideas but cutting words which do not work to carry ideas. Strive for less words and more ideas, this is a good guiding principle. Subtract words and keep doing so until you can no longer subtract any words without losing an idea.

The goal in following simplicity is to make every paragraph, sentence and even word *matter*. Simplicity means to ensure that every word is giving some form or color to the idea. Simplicity is not removing the idea but to ensure every word there adds to the idea, and removing only those words which do not add something to the idea already there.

When you simplify you clarify. Simplicity clarifies for by removing the unnecessary it leaves no distractions allowing the reader to see only one clear picture. Simplicity is eliminating all but the absolutely essential, to not just have the best and most precise words but to then cut out and eliminate any word which does not serve your purpose. In writing as in life you should never allow any element of the purposeless into it.

Clarity in style is often hindered in a work by having too many superfluous words and sentences. A general flaw of writers is to use loaded sentences, one with too many objects, details, things going on, where *multiple* pictures form, overlap, contradict and distort one another. Be careful not to add too many layers to a sentence. A sentence like a building can collapse in upon itself under its own weight.

Too many words dilute the picture being drawn. An overabundance of words allows a reader to draw different pictures and meanings. The real meaning gets lost in the many differing meanings drawn by the words.

The more words you use to get your point across the more likely it is your point will get lost in all those words.

The terse writer in approaching his craft sees words as a valuable resource. As a valuable resource they are never to be wasted, never invested in unprofitable endeavors, each and every word used is to be employed in the manner that gives maximum profit. The terse writer versus the over writer are the result of two differing value scales, for the over writer the value he places upon words is not high enough, for he wastes words, whereas with the terse writer placing so high a value upon words he spends them only as necessary.

Style is largely a result of a writer's value judgments about words. The master of style from whom brilliance and beauty is the normal order of things his style emerges as it does because of the heights he moved words to upon his value scale, for the master stylist believes that words matter, for they are beautiful, each with its own nature, a nature which when used in the right way and place can literally transform a life, or even the whole world. For the master stylist to waste a word means one lacks a mastery of words.

Terseness is good because by removing the barrier of the unnecessary it allows all of our words to work together to achieve enough force to drive our point home.

Aspire to terseness or else you will become tedious. The tedious sense springs up when the reader feels that his time is being wasted, where he is still trying to get to a point which should have already have been made, and it is not unlikely the book will be thrown down before the point is made, or if finally made it is no longer cared about.

If the reader can skip over a sentence or paragraph without losing anything of the meaning or the spirit of the writing then such parts are a waste and should be cut out.

No description for the sake of description. Do not spend a whole paragraph describing a setting, a person etc. unless such description adds something meaningful to the work. Keep style the servant of idea.

The time in which words need to be cut is when their use does not add up to anything, where they do not clarify or add to the effect or have any impact.

Good writing is often achieved through a Spartan spirit so learn how to say much with few words.

Driving straight to your point ensures no one gets lost.

In writing do not let your pen depart from your purpose. Do not get lost while writing in the superfluous, unimportant side issues, rambling, and using pretty words which serve no end.

Do not use throwaway sentences or paragraphs. Value your writing enough not to make it disposable. Do not leave in your work parts that should have been thrown into the editing trash can lest you encourage the reader to toss your work into the actual trash can

Insipid pleasantries may belong in a conversation but not in a book. Literary works are the proper stage for the epic and heroic, not the commonplace and the mundane. (Who do not even deserve a stage.)

Do not include in a work apologies, silliness or nonsense. Do not detract from the sum of your writing by adding in negative elements.

The serious writer does not use throw away words. The inspiring writer does not allow the mundane to creep into his style and by invoking boredom lose his grip on the mind. The meaningful writer does not allow in the pointless lest it conceal the meaningful. The beautiful stylist does not allow nonsense, triteness, insipid pleasantries, or other such similar ugly literary vices to detract from his works, for he knows how to use words to create real beauty.

Mediocrity is no way to start, carry through or finish anything.

To avoid these types of common mistakes use the idea of cutting and compression. Cutting is eliminating completely useless words and sentences and paragraphs. Compression is cutting down two or more sentences or paragraphs that draw virtually the same picture into one. The goal of editing is to eliminate anything which does not aid in drawing clear pictures.

Editing your work can be as important as the writing of it. As you edit your work realize that every page, paragraph and even word must work towards achieving your desired end, and that anything which does not contribute towards achieving that end should be eliminated. Style must always serve the idea and be cut as need be to suit the idea. Edit all of your work very carefully and very coldly. When you edit your work you should do so in the same spirit that a cold blooded murderer has towards his work. You need to be ruthless in cutting out your own words.

Do not keep favorite phases or lines if they do not really belong there and just muddy things up. (If you find yourself having a hard time cutting out the really good lines then try this mind trick, create a throw away file, take the cut lines and write them down and keep them somewhere. This way while cutting the line out of the work you do not get the sense you are wasting it, just storing it away for later use.)

In editing leave only the living lines, cut out the dead. Like a gardener weeding cut away every single killing weed even if you only end up with a single flower; better one beautiful flower to gaze at than a large rotting mess that covers up the one beautiful thing.

An hour of writing often leads to several days of revising. (Sometimes months or even years). Accept the fact that the writer is going to create a great amount of work for the editor. When writing let the writer spew out words but then let the editor in to clean up the mess. Separate the writer and the editor; this is the only way each will be able to do their jobs. Fail to separate the writer from the editor and they will engage in a literary wrestling match, and the work will be hurt by the fight. Do not let the editor stop the writer from pouring forth words, nor let the writer stop the editor from cutting the unnecessary words.

Remember when editing that one paragraph clear and well written accomplishes more than ten paragraphs that are muddy and unclear.

Do not use ten paragraphs to say what could be just as clearly said in one or two paragraphs. Do not use ten adjectives if one or two clearly conveys your meaning.

Use bold ideas, startling assertions and high ideals expressed clearly and simply through ear catching, heart stopping soul inspiring phases that thru visual imagery grab hold of the mind and do not let go—*this* is word-painting.

The opposite forms of style— the blank page and the muddy styles

What you want to avoid in style is the non-visual or blank page and the muddy styles.

A non-visual stylist uses words but not images thru or in his words. This is the blank page artist, you see words but no visual images are drawn from them. For example he will use labels like beauty or evil without drawing up an image of what they are to him. The blank page artist fills the pages with words but does not fill the mind with images; the mind is what remains a blank page. The non-visual writer in describing the wall a tyranny has erected around its people might say something like the people are restricted by a barrier he would not draw up a visual image by saying an iron curtain has descended.

The blank page writer often labels, giving a tag to his idea to describe it but not actually drawing up a picture of it. He does not create depth thru description, draw up images, employ symbols, use metaphors, compare differing aspects of reality. The entity or idea he is describing is not given shape to. He has no image on which to hang his idea. He gives things a label and goes no further.

The non-visual writer often uses short declarative sentences. Such as he ate the apple. Although this gives us an idea of what is happening it gives us no idea of what it looks like. What does the person look like? What does the apple look like? What is their spirit like? In simple declarative sentences what is missing is form and color and life.

Blank page writers or either lazy or weak writers, those who cannot give form or color to their writing forcing the reader to fill in the blanks. (For example when someone says it was a beautiful night, this is weak and lazy writing; *why* was it beautiful?)

The blank page stylist does not use imagery in his words; he for example would just say secrecy rather than say a veil has been drawn over things.

The blank page is writing without any flourish, black and white as opposed to color, words without any spirit, action, life, where being stripped of such things they are boring to read. The difference between word-painting and the non-visual blank page style is the difference between viewing the living and the dead. The word-painting style is colorful and pulsing and alive, where the non-visual style is empty, cold, dead. (The difference between a great novel and an instructional manual.)

Blank page writing is manual writing, as interesting to read as an instruction manual. There may be ideas there but a beautiful artistic style of visual imagery is missing. The non-visual writing does not have beauty flowing out of the words.

The blank page style commits one of the worst literary crimes of all, it is boring, boring not because it lacks ideas but has no spirit in presenting them. As one reads this non-visual style boredom builds and its consequence of revulsion follows and these feelings may become so strong that the emotions may deter the intellect, the book is thrown down in disgust, and the ideas it had to offer are lost. Even if the mind can endure the book with the right idea poorly presented it gains the idea through a process of literary torture. For an example of the non-visual boring style refer to the manner in which most philosophers write.

The blank page style could also be called eye glazing writing, for this describes the psychological and physical effects boring writing can have on the eyes, causing them to glaze over and the mind's eye with nothing interesting to focus on wanders away.

The non-visual may have the right ideas but has no spirit in expressing them. Without spirit the reader's mind is left unmoved, and fails to see any pictures. The word-painting style awakens the human spirit by exciting it with beautiful literary imagery opening it up to seeing the values offered through the writing.

The blank page stylist often denounces the ideal of majestic writing, of writing not just of elevated ideals but also with an elevated style. They resort to one of the ugliest forms of self-justification—the common man argument. The common man does not talk like this say these mediocrity justifiers. This is exactly why we need majestic writing, to inspire and uplift us to our highest potential in a way ordinary everyday language cannot achieve.

Muddy writing is when we delve into a writer's work and can find no clear picture of his meaning. The words do not draw pictures, instead they conceal them. Muddy writing is when a reader plows through a paragraph and no clear picture emerges and thus no clear meaning is reaped. The reader in plowing through such muddy literary fields ends up saying the word that shows a failure in style, the word what?? What did he mean by that? What is he trying to say? What does he want me to think? If a rational and reasonably intelligent person leaves a book with a string of what's, where the only thing he reaped was confusion then this is a literary failure, a style that falls short of achieving the purpose of writing, to communicate ideas through words.

The muddy writer in describing a tyranny might say things are restrictive rather than say an iron curtain has descended; this is muddy writing, for it begs the question what does restrictive mean? Restrictive can have many meanings whereas an iron curtain has a clear meaning.

Muddy writing is the style that creates a labyrinth in words, where the mind wanders through a maze of words seeking to find a clear picture, and either cannot work its way through the maze of words to find it, or else all the twists and turns ensure that what is found is a distorted picture.

The muddy writer often uses mixed metaphors, contradictory imagery, images that have multiple meanings.

Oftentimes the muddy writer words do not match the spirit of what is being described. Using small words to describe larger than life people, great words to describe small people. The spirit of the words must match the spirit of the idea being discussed. For example if describing what is to you a beautiful skyscraper you would not describe it as a gray, grimy goliath but as a soaring, elegant glass clad giant.

A hero cannot be described with metaphors like scurrying around like a cockroach for this is muddy writing, he must be described in the terms appropriate to a hero. (He led like a lion). The image cannot contradict the idea.

Many strip the life out of words. Some do it by accident; they do not know how to inject spirit into their style. Some do it on purpose; they use innocuous words not to reveal but to conceal harsh realities or unpleasant truths.

Many use concealing language on purpose. For example a politician describing the killing of civilians as "collateral damage." His goal in using a term like collateral damage is to ensure no pictures are being drawn and thus no emotions are being aroused.

Oftentimes what causes a writer to become muddy in his writing is when he becomes emotional rather than rational in his style of expression. In this case he does not express himself clearly, and writes in a way as if he assumes his readers have a method other than reason to see what he means. For example in describing a city the muddy writer will describe how it makes them feel as if you are supposed to understand from their emotional reactions to the city what it is like yet this leaves you with no idea of what the city is actually like. Emotions though are not guides to reality. People can react emotionally to the same thing in different ways. This is a failure for the writer for he is describing only his reactions to reality and not reality itself.

Oftentimes muddy writers are so because they are not loyal to facts, and morally do not see the need for any reason to be loyal to them. Of course some writers do not have anything worth saying, and muddy up their writing to hide the fact of its lack of worth. Worst of all are the writers who have something indecent to say and muddy their writing up to hide the fact of their indecency.

Another example of muddy writing is literary waffling, using words like sort of, possibly, maybe, words that refuse to stand for anything. By waffling the writer is trying to draw a picture which does not really show anything. Waffling is a result of a writer afraid to say clearly what it is he stands for. Waffling is not a lacking in literary skill but a lacking in moral courage. Have the courage of your convictions when writing. Spineless writing is as unappealing as a spineless person.

With a poorly written work even a person who likes to read will be unable to keep their eyes on the pages. With a well written work even a person who normally is not a fan of reading will not be able to peel his eyes away from the pages.

Word painting transports the reader into your literary world. The non-illustrative writer does not transport you anywhere. The muddy writer leaves you lost.

With the poor writer you cannot draw pictures from his words.

With the good writer you can see a picture. With the great writer you can see yourself in his picture and the picture becomes a part of you.

Well written literary works are not easily written. To achieve excellence in style requires a willingness to write and then rewrite (or redraw) something ten, twenty, even a hundred times or more. For clear and thus beautiful literary pictures to emerge will often requires vast amounts of time, vast amounts of frustration and vast amounts of wadded up paper. It is hard work word-painting to perfection yet to end up viewing a perfect literary picture makes it all worth it. Do not accept literary pictures that are blurry or a blank boring page of just words, instead keep writing and rewriting each paragraph until clear and thus beautiful literary pictures burst forth with life from the pages.

Word-painting is not something you use in every sentence or paragraph. (Particularly in writing dialogue). Word-painting may just use a single word in a paragraph to give it a symbol or image. Sometimes word-painting keeps returning to an image. Sometimes it is a single photograph surrounded by many paragraphs. Sometimes the visual imagery becomes predominant, a whole work shot thru with images.

Word-painting is not simply adding in a metaphor here or an adjective there. It is these things but so much more; this is a style that creates literary pictures creating thought thru the pictures, moving into the mind and moving it to action, not just because of what is being expressed but also because of the manner of expressing it. Word-painting is the difference between a cheap dime novel and great art. The difference between a mundane style and a Shakespearean grandeur. A great style like a great idea can move the mind; the two together become an irresistible force.

An example of word-painting

Here is an example of word-painting from Winston Churchill's famous iron curtain speech, and in which I will contrast his heroic spirit expressed in an illustrative style of expression with a non-illustrative and a muddy bureaucratic manner of expression. From Winston

Churchill—"From Stettin in the Baltic to Trieste in the Adriatic, an iron curtain has descended across the continent." The muddy style of saying the same thing—"On the continent things are somewhat restrictive." Note the first quote from Churchill is objective, uncompromising, and in his use of the term iron curtain describes in a very illustrative term the actual nature of how the Soviet government was literally penning its people in. Churchill's manner of speaking also shows a morally courageous and defiant spirit in standing up to the evil. The second is unclear as to what is exactly happening, and by waffling is a form of moral cowardice.

The non-visual way of saying it—"A barrier has been erected on the continent." Although this describes what is happening there is something lacking in it, what it lacks is the startling visual imagery that Churchill drew. A barrier is a label and has no clear meaning. What kind of barrier? A barrier can mean many things whereas an iron curtain draws a clear cut picture.

6

Passion—
Writing with Your Soul on Fire

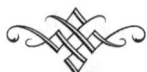

All great artists are fired by passion, and out of the fire of their passion their art is created. In the fire of passion is the spark which unleashes the creative force of man. The passionate unleashing of the creative force causes a violent explosion onto the written page. Fiery passion more than unleashing the creative force shapes it as it comes out, giving the molten force the ideal form. To write with passion is to write with your soul on fire.

Passion as a principle is the deliberate and directed unleashing of the creative energy. To write the words which have the fire you must first set yourself on fire.

The writer to create must first be stoked with passion, a passion for the written word, for the passionate search for the right word, with a passionate belief in the power and divine mission of the written word, and from all this passion is stoked and unleashed the creative powers.

The universe itself was created from the unleashing of a fiery creative energy, and so too is art. Indeed the unleashing of the creative force of the artist is essentially unleashing the same kind of creative force from which this glorious universe was created; the creative process of the artist is an explosion, a creative big bang which brings forth new worlds.

Here is how I see my creative process—it all begins in the primal idea, an idea which builds in fury and power, a passionate will builds within to unleash it, will and energy now raging to be unleashed, the violent raging of passionate forces builds to a cataclysmic force, finally the force can no longer be contained, there is a passionate explosion, the creative fury is unleashed, fiery energy bursts onto the page, the creative torrent pours out, from this swirling fury a new universe explodes into existence: fiery suns light up, new worlds form, and life comes into being. *This* is what passion is, not some contenting pastime but the unleashing of a violent fury that you could not contain even if you wanted to.

The true artist creates because he is spiritually seized; the artist's soul becomes seized by a fiery passion, this fiery force growing within him until it is too intense for any other thing to stand with, this passion feeding him and feeding on him, and the artist unleashes his fiery passion into the art, not because he wants to but because he has to, for he has no choice but to quench the soul burning passion. The soul possessed by a fiery passion to create, because it *must* create, this is the furnace from which all great art emerges. All great art flows from the fiery furnace of passion. From the heat of passion art and life are created.

Passion impregnates the creative soul. A passion for art and for doing the art creates the fertile ground from which art is born. Without passion the soul is a barren desert from which nothing grows. Trying to bring great art from a passionless soul is like trying to grow a flower in the desert.

While a universe can be created only when certain natural forces occur an artist can create a beautiful universe when and as he wills it if he knows how to create the force of passion.

Passion is to be consumed by a desire for something. Passion as an artistic principle is to deliberately unleash that desire into creative endeavors.

Where the spark for the fire of passion comes from—from the mind which holds the idea of the importance of doing this and from the heart in the joy of doing it; mind and heart united together create the fire of passion in the human spirit.

The formula for passion in creating art—meaning= passion= joy, and these three together make the work *worth* doing.

Passion applied to writing is to have an all consuming burning love for writing, caused by the knowledge that when writing you are doing exactly with your life what you know you should be doing with it, a consequence of the belief of the importance of why it should be done and why you should be the one doing it, an emotional state that is the result of rational convictions, these passionate convictions resulting in several important consequences, causing a mental perspective resulting in a highly intense state of will to do it and focus upon doing it, this feeling creating that rational will and overpowering emotions whose intensity drive you to create, this passion initiating and sustaining the writing process, this passion which unleashes every inch of your being into the writing process, the passionate state reaching into you and drawing out a potential that cannot be touched when passion is lacking, this passion a joy that drives you to the work and drives out of you your true potential, driving you to the fulfillment of your life's purpose, realizing a passionate joy that as it is poured out into the creative process is created anew in the form of a proud joy in witnessing the birth of a artistic creation and then achieving that deep sense of satisfaction in doing with life exactly what you want to do with it and doing it well.

Here I speak to you of making writing more than a pastime, more than a way to make a living, here I speak of making writing a way of life, of making writing the art of *being alive*.

Just as a sculptor to be good must love the touch and feel of stone so to a writer to be good must be in love with words. The writer loves words the way a lover loves his romantic partner; the lover worships the bodily form of his beloved for in it is what he loves most. The writer loves words for in every word is contained an idea.

Passion for writing is ultimately a passion for the creative process, both in its results and in the process itself.

There are many benefits from approaching your writing fired up with passion for it. The need for passion arises in what it can do to the writing and what it can do to you. The following are the reasons why passion is a needed creative principle.

Passion starts the creative process—To jump start and begin the creative process is for many the most difficult barrier in creating and sometimes an insurmountable one. For the passionate artist beginning the creative process is not a barrier to struggle over but taking the easy step into a joyful heaven. Passion is needed for the creative process for it is often what causes the whole creative process to begin in the first place.

You do not have to push a kid to play, and neither do you need to push someone to do that which he is passionate about. Those fired by passion rush to do that which they are passionate about whenever the chance presents itself. Indeed the passion driven always steer things so the chance is always being presented. Passion is an important creative principle because it is often the spark that fires the writer to create in the first place.

Some writers to make up for a lack of passion make discipline their principle. To have an all consuming passion for what you do renders any need for discipline superfluous, for in such a state one does it not because they have to but because they want to, and so it is no effort to make the effort to do it. Do you find a need to discipline yourself to eat your favorite food, to listen to your favorite music, to dance for joy, for these things inspire passion and are rushed into whenever the opportunity presents itself. Find equal passion in doing your writing that you have for all the great joys and you will be the most disciplined writer in the world although it will not seem so to you. With discipline you write when you have to, with passion you write whenever you can; this over time makes for a big difference in how often you write.

Passion sustains the writing process—The passionate do what they are passionate about for as long as body and spirit are capable. Here passion aids in creating greatness because 1—it keeps the passionate working longer and producing more and 2—it also raises their skill in producing since they do it so much and for so long. With discipline you do as little as discipline demands, with passion you do as much as you possibly can; this over time makes for a big difference in how much you write.

Passion channels the human potential into the creative process—The man when passionate about what he is doing and why he is doing it the whole soul is focused on what it is doing, the human potential is touched and unleashed, and the work catches this unleashing of the human potential. Passion causes you not just to put in the time to doing something but to put all of yourself into the time you are doing it. Passion over time makes for a big difference in the quality of what you write.

The need for passion to be applied to your writing lies in the fact that writing is a *rational process,* therefore only the mind fully focused on the process will be capable of doing it well. Passion unleashes the full power of your mind onto the written page because passion focuses all of your being onto the writing, where the belief in the importance of what you are doing and the passion for doing it makes the mind unable to focus on other lesser things.

The meaning of being focused in writing is this, when writing you do not think of the outside world, the page in front of you is the whole world. True focus occurs when nothing exists but the thing you are doing.

The mind becomes truly focused only when it believes nothing is more important than the thing in front of it, and then all other things fade into insignificance beside it.

An artist to create must immerse himself completely into the creative process He must be there both in body and spirit. Any part of his mind not immersed in the process becomes a cord pulling the writer back, keeping from arriving at the idea and the image, the way and the words.

While discipline may put the body into the writer's chair it cannot put the mind. A writer may have his body in the chair and his mind may be a thousand miles away. Discipline can put a part of you but not your whole being into the creative act. Only passion can put all of you into the work and all of you into the fiery state needed to do the work.

There are those times when a writer writes where on the wings of passion he ascends into a zone of higher consciousness, that place where he is fully conscious but no longer self-conscious, where he loses all awareness of everything but the creative process, where while in such a zone he knows exactly what he wants to say, and is always choosing the best words to say what he wants to say, knowing on some subconscious level that he is doing great work, in a state of complete focus and complete joy. It is moments like these that are what true artists live for—to be doing exactly what you want to be doing and doing it in the best way possible. This kind of state can only come from a passionate love for what you are doing, in the why you are doing it and the actual process of doing it. Only passion can lock a man into this state; the pain of a dreary discipline only bars him from it.

Focus is like a volume control. You can turn it up or turn it down. Turn it up to full. The danger of turning down your focus results in what I call the one times twenty rule, for every one percent of focus you lose you lose times twenty in the quality of your writing. Even a two percent loss can result in a loss of forty percent of the quality of your writing.

When you lose focus in your writing you either lose sight of your destination or idea and drift away or else use the wrong means and find yourself being steered poorly in your use of words.

While you can and should be emotional about the creative process and even while engaged in the process you should not allow the emotions to override the intellect. Let your emotions drive you but let reason steer. Writing with passion does not mean you switch off your mind while writing. *Writing is an intellectual process, emotions are allowed only when they aid the process.* In using the word passion here I am talking about something that results from *rational convictions,* and is *transmitted in rational terms.* In being emotional about writing the emotions comes from rational thought, which give to you a sense of intense emotional fire, and this then should be used to fire up your mind for writing, yet what you must not do is allow these emotions to take the place of thought; burning emotions must be used to fire you to think harder.

Passion puts the fire in the writing—When the writer is truly and even painfully passionate about his writing he writes with his soul on fire, and this burning passion transmits itself onto the written page. When you read a work written by such a man in such a state you do not just skim over his words but the power of his writing burns itself into your soul. Passion translates into writing that is more alive, where the writer's spirit expresses itself in words that are glowing from the fire, where it is a fiery joy to read for the spirit of the writing then burns in you. Passion puts not just intellect but also feeling into the words.

Passion finds joy in the creative process itself—The writer passionate about creating gets joy from the very process of creating itself, for he thinks creating is a value in and of itself. To create in a state of violent passion makes creating art more than a means of glorifying life *it is life*; creating the most intense state of being alive.

For the true artist his art is not something he does it is what he is. The art and his life are one and the same thing; he lives for the art, the art the living expression of what he is. A true artist makes art more than a way to make a living, it is living itself. He makes his art his life, and devotes his life to his art. A life devoted to art, an art devoted to life.

The passionate writer gains joy from the writing process itself. The writer passionate about writing is ultimately passionate about rational expression, as thru the writing he is fulfilling himself. Before, doing and after the writing he thinks to himself this matters, my life matters, the work I am doing with my life makes my life worth living. The creative act is the highest human act, man becoming a kind of God.

The man passionate about what he does finds the working process being the equivalent of a walk thru a Garden of Eden with many fruits lying thru it.

By approaching your writing fired up by a sense of passion you make the writing process more enjoyable while doing it and the writing better reading when it is done.

Write from a passion for both the purpose and the process of writing. This passion makes it possible to engage in the process of writing necessary to fulfill the purpose of writing.

There are many out there whom I call daydream writers. A daydream writer is one who desires to write but does not sit down and actually write. While the passionate writer burns through his pages day after day the daydream writer writes nothing for he lacking the passion is unable to light his creative fuse. He will always remain a daydream writer until he finds a way to ignite his passion. The daydream writer or the daydreamer in any field occurs when they desire the results or rewards of the process but cannot find joy in the process itself. The long desert of passionless work that stretches before them renders them unwilling to travel it to get to the reward that lies on the other end.

For the passionate artist the creative journey is the greatest reward with more rewards lying at its end. Those who find no joy in the artistic journey will usually find themselves unable to take it; and if they do take it they will regret it.

Some writers treat every day of writing like the first day of a passionate romance, where everything and every moment is new and exciting, where they rush into their love with excitement, wonder, awe and joy.

And some writers treat their writing as a worn out marriage, loveless, joyless, where everything and every moment is boring, for it has all been done before, and done too many times before, wanting to divorce it but knowing nowhere better to go and so sticking on with it for the worse.

Writing like any form of art is often described as an agony and an ecstasy. When you approach your writing fired by a passion for it the agony mostly dissipates and the ecstasy increases many times over.

The writers without passion, or the agony school

Now we have arrived at the opposite school of thought on writing, the agony school. The agony school is for those who lack the passion for writing, those who do not make passion an *artistic principle*. Without passion for what one is doing one finds only agony in the doing of it. The agony school may not necessarily make agony a creative principle, only accepts it as an unavoidable part of the creative process. Many writers have described the writing process as boring drudgery, as *agony*. These kind seem to lack the fire of passion for what they do, lacking a passion for what they produce or else for the process of producing it. Many regard the creative process of art as a cross to be borne rather than the wings to joyfully soar on.

Those who lack the passion, those who have nothing burning within them are the ice cold writers. Those artist who are cold to the creative process, who lack the fiery spirit, find from the icy chill of their spirit when they take a creative journey it is an agonizing walk thru a cold hell with no heavenly rewards at its end.

There are two reasons why writers lack the passion. The one type of passionless writer cannot find passion in the *goal* of writing; he may enjoy toying with words and building word structures but such wordplay will never build up to anything meaningful for him. The other kind of passionless writer does not have any passion for the *process* of writing. He in seeing the long stretch of creative writing ahead of him sees not a chance to walk thru a Garden of Eden but a long barren stretch of desert he has to take a monotonous journey thru. In both cases there is no meaning, in the goal and/or the process, thus they lack the passion, thus they lack the joy; and out of this void of meaninglessness and boredom the monster of agony attacks.

Some artists seem to outright hate the creative process, while many others fail to gain any real enjoyment from it. Here they make their life path one lined with the weeds of boredom and drudgery. My advice is to either change their point of view so their path seems like a walk thru a Garden of Eden, or else if unable to change their view then change their path in life so it is one they do not hate walking upon.

Being an artist is a way of life, and should be pursued only by those who burn with a passion for living the life of the artist. Art is really meant only for those who would be miserable without it, and for anyone else who is not meant for art but takes up art will find themselves miserable *because* of the art.

The consequences of accepting the agony point of view are

immense. First off it may kill the creative process altogether before it has even begun. It is human nature to avoid altogether that which causes us pain. The agony writer often cannot even find the will to sit down and write. Agony is a whip that drives the writer from his chair.

Agony torturing the writer thru the creative process shortens it, lessening the time and degree of it, usually to the point where the artist's pain of guilt in not truly applying himself is less than the pain of fully applying himself.

Agony destroys the bridge to your true potential because agony focuses the mind from the work onto the agony itself.

Agony snuffs the human fire out. Lacking passion the disciplined writer may produce as many words as the passionately driven one yet his words like himself will lack the fire.

You writers without any passion for writing how do you expect to light up your pages when you have no fire within you?

Allow your writing or anything to become a source of pain to you and you will find ways to avoid doing it, spend less time doing it when you do force yourself to do it, and will not throw your whole being into doing it and in the end you will not feel any satisfaction as you hold that inferior work in your hand that only reminds you you are not doing with your life what you should be.

There are passionless writers who not willingly drawn to their writing desk try to make up for it by enforcing a dreary discipline upon themselves to painfully drive them to their desk. A writer who makes discipline his principle makes discipline *the chains* which bind him and like any slave will seek any chance to break the chains which bind him. The chains of discipline when borne only forces the artist who bears them to undergo a dreary torture, and the artist without passion will either give up, or else keep doing the work which will slowly kill his spirit and produce a work without any spirit. Without passion for what you are doing discipline is ultimately an exercise in futility. An enforced discipline in a joyless profession is ultimately a dangerous act. To spend your life doing what you lack a passion for doing will kill a little bit of your soul every time you do it.

Discipline is forcing yourself to do something you do not want to do; discipline then gives you no joy in the doing.

The passionless writer does not feel alive while creating; for him life is put on hold while working, he comes back from the writing feeling a little bit dead.

The writer who lacks the passion for his writing sees his writing still born, lifeless words that reflect the spirit that wrote them. He is often unable to focus his mind on what he is doing, and allows his pen to drift from his point, and sees his style emerge muddy and unclear. Oftentimes he cannot even write, as his revulsion at doing what is to him a dreary duty often renders him unable to even sit down to write. In the end regardless of what is produced, or not produced, or badly produced he finds himself trapped in a joyless life, and defeats the ultimate purpose of writing, to transmit thru art the life-affirming spirit, both in the art and the artistic process itself.

The agony of discipline puts the creative seeds in a grim soil and casts over it a dark light, and neither joyful art nor joy as such grows from this environment. Passion puts the creative process in a fertile soil and casts it in a bright happy light, and from this environment grows both joyful art and a joyful artist growing until it becomes an artistic paradise.

In upholding passion as a principle and denouncing discipline this is not denouncing having set times for writing, of following a writing schedule, what this is about is the *mental context* with which you approach the times that you do write—do you regard it as a burning pleasure or a boring duty? It is not imposing a schedule that is the problem it is imposing the idea of it being a boring agonizing thing to be endured on a regular basis that is where discipline becomes a bad thing. Passion is about turning the creative process (scheduled or not) into both a meaningful and joyful thing as the necessary means to be able to engage successfully in it.

When you have found your life's great passion you do not schedule your passion into your life you schedule your life around your passion.

Why do some lack the fire within? As I said they cannot find any passion in either the goal and/or the process of writing. For those whom writing is only an agony perhaps such kind spend their times writing only what others want them to write. (Meaning they lack artistic integrity.) In this case such kind lacks passion for their work because they do not care for the actual work. I too would hate writing if in doing it I did not care about what I was writing about. Or perhaps they write about humans who are depraved or evil in their works, spending their time glorifying the evil men and their evil acts which make their art evil as well. Depicting men whose souls are sewers such kind are often turned off by the very smell of their own creations. (Meaning they lack the principle of idealism.) Of course such kind lack a passion for writing, they hate the end result of it. I too would hate writing if I spent all of my time using my best to depict the worst in man. Then there are the trifling artists who write of worthless men and their worthless lives, making their art worthless as well. Knowing the end result of their work is without value to them or anyone they fail to feel the fire of passion for their efforts. (They also lack the principle of idealism.) I too would hate writing if in doing it I knew it had no significance. In some cases a writer fails to approach the writing process with the right system for writing making their writing always a mess and therefore always an agony. (Those who do not know to word-paint.) Writing too would be an agony for me if I had the right goal but had no way there. In all of these cases it is their perspective, their way of thinking about writing and its goals and the process of achieving that goal, which dooms them to agony.

Many do become writers for the wrong reasons. They hold the wrong why, and because they are not in the art for the art itself often see the actual creative process turn into an endurance trial of drudgery and boredom. Many write for fame, money, prestige, to perform what they regard as a social duty, and these are all wrong reasons to write. Writing is an art form, a field that should be open only to those with a passionate need to express their mind and its own values, to express the value and joy of being alive, who love the creative process as the essence of being alive, since it is a rational expression of their mind and its ideas and values and of their mind's value. Writing should be done full time only by those with something worth saying *and* who enjoy the process of saying it.

Writing can be an agony or an ecstasy. Writing if you come to it through passion is mostly ecstasy and only very rarely an agony. You should not write if writing is *only an agony.*

The reasons outlined here are not the only reasons why most people write, but they are the only reasons why you should write *if* you want to produce meaningful works *and* have a meaningful life in the writing field. Write only to satisfy a passionate burning within, write because you have the fire of a great idea in you that you wish to fire the world up with, write because you are passionately fired up by the writing process, because writing is a worthwhile thing in and of itself. By coming at your writing with such a mentality you will in time release the best of yourself onto the written page.

The passionate writer finds joy coming from every direction in the creative process—to find the right idea, to burn within to unleash it into the written page, to have that passionate outburst, to create a new artistic world, to edit and shape it into a perfect world, to then reap the greatest reward as he sees his idea reflected back to him in a world where all is as it should be and says to himself I did it; for him from beginning to end nothing but pure joy. The passionate writer finds his greatest passion and joy in being a creator and finds it is thru his art his passion is both fed and satisfied.

I myself since I feel the end goal of writing is so important would be willing to suffer for it yet luckily there is absolutely no need to suffer, since my philosophy on writing makes it a joy. It is this philosophy of the value and joy of artistic creation that makes it possible to engage in artistic creation.

All you have to do to write is create the right mental perspective on writing, declare it to be meaningful and a joy because it is so meaningful in so many ways, and you can then achieve the end goal of writing without having to suffer to get there and can fully enjoy the process of getting there; and it is only by enjoying the process of creating art that you will get there.

You artist, you fools, who speak of the need to suffer for your art if you wish to create great art you must learn to be deliriously happy for your art.

If you cannot find a passionate joy in what you do then create the thoughts that turn what you do into joy. If you lack and cannot acquire the passion for writing *then do not write.* Do not waste your life doing what you do not want to do. Far too many other humans do that already. Do not be one of those fools who when he has the ability to make life into an ecstasy and instead through his choices turns it into an agony.

Passion the result of mental perspective

Passion is not something you are born with, or given, you must stoke your own passion. You must learn how to spark the fire of passion.

What creates joy or agony in writing or in anything you do does not really lie in the nature of the thing you are doing but in the nature of the mentality or perspective in which you approach it. Mental perspective is what really creates the agony or ecstasy in anything. How you frame something determines how you see it.

The joy or misery you experience in anything comes not really from the activity itself but from the mental perspective from which you approach it.

You can take two men and have them perform the exact same job—the one loves doing the job, the other hates it. Both are doing the exact same job yet have exactly opposite emotions about it and the difference between the two lies in perspective, one for certain reasons has learned to value and enjoy the work, the other for different or even the same reasons has taught himself to despise doing the work. Through differing mental perspective's one has created ecstasy from his work, the other because of his mental perspective can take only agony from his time doing the work.

The thought of poking into the bloody insides of a human body will fill a surgeon with passion and cause the average person to faint; such is the power of perspective.

Mental perspective or the value judgments you place on certain things are really what determines how you feel about them. Art, work, lifestyles, life itself, whether you are attracted to or repulsed by something depends on your perspective on it. You value the things you value because you believe you should value them, and the things that repulse you do so because you believe they are of no value to you.

Since passion for something is not innate, it is something you learn, and being a writer is a way of life, for those who choose to be writers you must learn how to create a passion for your chosen way of life. You must learn how to burn.

To cultivate a passion for writing you must hold within you four beliefs or value judgments, you must 1—have a passion for ideas and believe in the importance of them, 2—know that the goal of writing is to capture and transmit important ideas 3—have a passion for the process of writing, believing in the importance of rational exercise and expression as a value in and of itself and 4—hold a deep belief in the importance of writing to your life and all human life. (Which is the sum of holding the first three beliefs.)

What should first turn someone to writing or else keep them there after turning to it is a deep belief in the importance of ideas. A writer begins to cultivate a passion for his life's work by dedicating it to a goal that has value and meaning to them; to not just write but to write for a reason that is worth it. Man to survive and flourish at life needs knowledge of the right ideas for human living. Those who are in love with life and realize the importance of ideas to life through these beliefs acquire a passion for learning and knowing about the ideas needed for life, the ideas that make life worth living. By believing in the importance of ideas as such when you approach your writing you are simply transferring this passionate belief into the goal of your writing, and therefore making it a goal that then matters to you, making it something that is of the highest importance to you, and your perspective then works to create a passion for achieving the ultimate goal of writing, of capturing and expressing the ideas that matter in human living.

To write from the deep belief in the importance of ideas means you are not merely writing silly stories to kill time, or babbling on in some essay, you are speaking of the deepest most important things of life, and the very attempt to do so gives your life the deepest meaning.

Passion must not just be for the writing process itself but must also be for the subject matter you are writing about. I stated that the goal of writing is to capture and present the ideas that matter in human living. This is a general principle. In applying it to your particular case this means that you should capture and present the ideas that *matter the most to you.* My advice to writers in choosing their subject matter is to write about the particular ideas that get your blood boiling. In choosing your subject you should do so by saying this is what matters most to me, and so therefore I will write about it. While anything which is of value to human living is a worthy subject for writing about only some ideas are worthy subjects for writing about *for you.* In choosing your subject you are not just writing about any ideas but the ones you feel the most deeply about, in your belief in their importance to human life and in your passion generated while writing about such important ideas.

The writer in choosing his subject matter must journey deep into himself, into the place of deepest meaning, the place of his most blazing thoughts, *into the things which burn him most,* for this is where the fire lies, and draw his ideas for writing from the fiery passionate core of his being. Only thru writing from what burns you within will you be able to create the work that has the fire in it.

The artist is possessed by a vision which he then creates in an artistic form so others can be possessed by it.

For example freedom is one of man's highest values, and political science a very worthy subject to write about; yet if the idea of political science bores you, if you cannot stand writing about it then political science is not a worthy subject for you in particular to write about. Now if you burn on the inside about freedom, if you cannot stop yourself from thinking about or talking about this subject, if you cannot understand why more men do not value freedom as highly as what you do, then this passionate feeling on the inside tells you what you should be writing about. This passion for the idea will be not just for the importance of the idea in actual life but will also translate into a passion for writing about it, and that passion for it will show in the burning words you write.

To be passionate about writing you must write what you are passionate about. Write from your greatest loves and hates.

Man survives physically and morally through a process of reason. Those who realize this and value living come to value the use and exercise of their minds in and of itself. To cultivate a passion not just for the goal of writing but in the writing itself you must cultivate a passion for exercising your mind. Only those who aspire to mindlessness dread using their minds. If you wish to be a fully developed human being who is empowered to live life to the fullest you must learn to value using your mind to the fullest. Writing is a rational process, one that when done under the right premises will tax your mind to its fullest, and to make this process an ecstasy rather than an agony you must learn to relish the process of using your mind, which begins by believing in the importance of using your mind fully, and only then you will find joy in the full exercise of your mind.

In writing from the belief of the high value of employing reason into the labor of the creative process itself fulfills the deepest meaning of life, for here you are a human living up to and fulfilling his highest potential.

A deep belief in the importance of writing, of what it can offer to you in the process and the end results of that process, of how writing can transform you and your life for the better, means that since you believe in the importance of it you will not regret the time you spend doing it, since this is something important, worth the time spent on it, since there is nothing or few things as important as this, that since the process of it is a joy and joy is the goal of man's life you will say this is the way I should be living my life, doing that which is so meaningful and thus such a joy to me.

Before writing actually work to psyche yourself up for the writing. Be like sports players before the big game. Mentally talk to yourself.

Psyche yourself up thru mental pep talks. Say to yourself yes it is time to write again, time to do something that matters, time to create something truly great. If you come to your work all psyched up the odds are good that that writing session will be both productive and enjoyable.

Whatever you do do not psyche yourself down. Do not approach your writing time saying oh no I have got to write again, I do not know why I write, it is not that important. Do this and a lot of the passion and as a consequence quality and joy of writing will vanish, your writing destroyed by your way of thinking about writing.

A mind in a single moment is capable of doing a complete turn around in thought. A mind seemingly defeated one moment can by having a single right thought triumph a moment later.

Unmotivated minds are unfocused minds, and being so cannot accomplish great feats of the mind. The greater the degree a person is unfocused the greater the limits placed on what they are capable of. This stands in stark contrast to the focused person, the passionate person, being so focused they can accomplish intellectual feats far beyond what the scatterbrained can do.

Your way of thinking about things deeply affects you in both what actions you perform and in the way you perform those actions. A person who continually psyched himself down will not care as deeply about his writing, often will not write at all, will not be as focused on it when he does write, and as a consequence will see what little he writes remain at an exceptionally mediocre level. A person psyched up for writing will come to care more deeply about his writing, and will write more often, will work longer and harder, will be many times more focused since he believes in the importance of writing and as the consequence of his attitude will raise the quality of his writing to exceptional heights.

For those artist who tend to think negatively about writing try this exercise for a week—try to have no negative thoughts about writing, talk to yourself as if you are one of the most important people who ever lived because you are a writer, say to yourself I matter because I am a writer. When it is time to write look forward to it, say yes it is time to create great things and to be truly alive and happy again. Allow no negative thoughts to enter your head. Do this for a week and see how much such an attitude transforms both you and your writing. I am sure that if you who lack the passion do transform your attitude it will make give you the fire about the worthy work you have dedicated your life to.

7

Artistic Integrity— My Art By My Standards

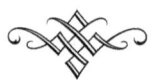

The great and glorious kingdom of art is always under siege by the forces of compromise. These barbaric forces seek to loot this glorious kingdom and leave it a desolate waste. The heroic artist raises the wall of artistic integrity around his artistic kingdom, protecting it from the rampaging forces of barbaric compromise, and his kingdom flourishes. In this essay lie the tools needed to defend yourself from the siege of artistic and moral compromise.

The principle and only meaning of artistic integrity—for me the artist the goal of my art lies in the art itself; my art done for my sake, done by my standards, because my art matters to me, and no other factor really matters to me. This statement represents the ideal of the true artist and the true and only meaning of artistic integrity. This ideal is the wall that is the moral defense that will protect you from the immoral siege of compromise.

In applying the principle of artistic integrity to your writing this means that in your choice of subject matter and how you present it that you will always make your art by your own highest artistic standards without weighing *any* other consideration. Editorial demands, social standards, current fads, public tastes, top selling lists, appeals to the lowest common denominator or any other denominator such outside standards cannot be allowed to play any part in setting your own standards for writing, for they will lower your standards from the highest they can be.

Integrity in adhering to your own artistic standards this means the highest standards possible, and not an inch less will do. It is not enough to just stay true to your own artistic vision your vision must be one worth staying true to. Artistic integrity becomes a high ideal only when you have a high vision for your art.

Art is about presenting the ideas that you believe in—this makes upholding artistic integrity more than a mere artistic matter, it makes it a matter of *moral conscience.*

Art is a intellectual and artistic discipline, but it is also far more than these, it is also a moral and religious one.

If you do not share and cannot share these convictions then you should leave the field of art, *or* at least be honest and admit that you are in it for the money or fame, admit that you as an artist have no convictions that stand above the bottom line or its immoral equivalent. The artist who makes his highest standard something like the bottom line can hold no high moral or artistic standards against it; such a man is not a true artist but a fame or money grubber who sells out his art and himself, posing as an artist in order to reap some outer reward of art.

Why make artistic integrity a principle that guides your writing? For only those who adhere to the highest standards produce any art of worth and are worth *anything* as artist *and as human beings.* A man like a literary work must have integrity to be worth anything.

To follow any standard other than the standard of artistic integrity means the selling out of the moral meaning of the art, and the selling out of the moral meaning of yourself as a human being.

In a previous essay I advised you to use writing as a means to express the highest values possible to man. The goal in integrity is to remain loyal to this ideal, using art as a means to elevate and exalt human existence. The ideal of artistic integrity ensures you express man's highest values without in any way, shape or form compromising this ideal to achieve some other desired goal or to conform to some other outer standard; because to have any other goal for your art is to make it impossible to achieve art's one true and highest goal.

In stating one must have integrity to the idealistic standard this is the only standard one can have moral loyalty to, as opposed to the trifling school whose sole standard is to have no high standards or the depravity school which moved by a hatred of man and of life its sole standard is the destruction of all human standards.

There are many different levels in writing to which the ideal of integrity must be applied to your writing. To have integrity in writing is not a one step thing, it is a multi-step thing stretching a vast distance. Artistic integrity must be defended on many levels, in the purpose of your writing, in how it is written, in who writes it, in publication etc. Integrity to your art means upholding your standards in every single element of the art *as an absolute*.

The sellout school of art

This standard of artistic integrity *as an absolute* separates me from the other school of writing, the sellout school. Now we must go to school to learn about an ugly aspect of the writing field, those who in their writing betray their artistic integrity, or the sellouts as I have marked them. An admittedly ugly but well deserved term. A sellout is a writer who sells out his artistic and moral standards *for any reason.*

An artist betrays his integrity when at any time for any reason he creates his art by any other standard other than his own personal highest artistic standards.

The sellout school is a school of thought which holds that there is *some reason* which justifies *betraying* your artistic standards; this means these is something you must hold *above* your own artistic and moral standards; this means you can hold no artistic standards against the reason why you are selling them out.

The sellout is he who writes for an audience of readers. Those who write for an audience do so with an eye on the rewards beyond the art itself and want an audience as the means to those rewards. In this case the art becomes a means to that audience and what that audience can do for the artist. The three things an artist is most likely to sell out for are the three F's—fortune, fame, fear. Fortune is any form of financial reward. Fame any sort of personal recognition (being famous, infamous, peer recognition, awards etc.) In the case of fortune the sellout wants the audience recognition as a means to its wallet; he who wants fame wants the audience recognition as an end in itself. In selling out because of fear this is betraying your art and yourself out of fear of how the audience may react to your true self expressed in the art.

Many artists keep an eye focused on the rewards beyond the art, seeing art as a means to some greater end. The true artist though sees the reward of art in the art itself.

The writer who writes for fame uses his art as a means to get people to talk about him; the writer who writes for money wants an audience so he can get paid by it. For the fame seeking artist and money grubbing artist the goal is number of books sold, not the worth of the books, the greater value is what men say about the books and not what worthwhile things the books actually has to say, what others think about you and not what you think about yourself. The money grubber makes the bottom line his highest value; the fame seeker essentially makes the recognition of other men his bottom line. In both cases the goal of the art lies beyond the art itself, in what it can make other people give to them and does not lie in the rewards of the art itself. In these cases the artist can hold no standards above the reason why he sold out, and the reasons why are so low this means essentially he can hold no real artistic standards whatsoever.

The sellout is anyone who writes to gain an audience. The artist of true integrity writes for an audience of one—himself. The writer who writes for an audience then makes what the audience wants to hear of greater importance than what he wants to say. The writer with artistic integrity thinks that what he has to say is the thing of greatest importance.

The rationales people give for selling out are many, one way or the other they all usually come back to being justified by the three F's. In freer societies people usually sell out for fortune or fame; in more repressive societies it is usually fear. (Repressive societies have little fortune or fame but have fear in abundance.) Now we must look at the rationales for selling out and see if they can stand up to reason.

The consequences of selling out

Selling out betrays you as a human being—First and foremost selling out yourself as an artist *also sells you out as a human being*. When a writer fails to follow the principle of artistic integrity in his writing it means he is no longer expressing his ideas and values; this is more than merely being silent about his values it represents the *betrayal* of his values. You cannot turn against your values and still hold your values. A writer may sell out for a variety of reasons, but regardless of the reason why when a writer betrays his moral values he betrays himself. In the moral weighing of selling out and why it adds up to a bad idea is it represents the sacrifice of greater values for lesser values. A sellout in exchange for fame, money, a spot on the top seller list, a penthouse suite etc. through his writing betrays and sells out his greatest values, his *moral values*, his self-respect, integrity, honesty, rationality, i.e. his soul. To not write about your ideas and values but what others want you to write is to replace your ideas and values for the ideas and values of those others. To sellout your moral principles thru your art is to more than merely betray them, it is to lose them completely as an artist and as a human being. A sellout is one who when he sits down to write says lets guess what will interest and excite other people, because those others are my standard of value, and I will write to appeal to them *without any regard to my own personal moral values*. In making any concession to the standards of others this requires you to drop *all* your own artistic and moral standards.

To adhere to the standards of others means *you can have no standards that are your own*. Even if in appealing to the masses makes a writer present high moral values the writer himself still has no moral values, he is a parrot who is just squawking whatever his masters want to hear as a means to another end without having any regard as to the nature of what is being said. This book is not intended as a course on ethics but let this ethical pronouncement be made in it, the man who surrenders his values, ideas and mind to squawk out whatever it is others want him to say for applause or a paycheck betrays himself as an artist and as a human being, and loses his moral self-worth. Such a man comes to realize that he is a moral slave to the opinions of others. Others pull his leash, and while the literary pet may be well paid or receive thunderous applause for his parroting the man who does this realizes that he is still just a pet leashed to the masses.

Artistic integrity is a liberating ideal for strict adherence to your own highest ideals is not a restriction but true freedom for it frees you to fly to wherever your mind feels is a worthy destination. It is quite liberating to not be chained to anyone for you are then able to say whatever you want. The sellout is a slave to others, for he is the one who ties himself by a chain to the mob he seeks to appeal to who then drags him around wherever it wants.

The artist who sells himself out is like the street walking whore selling himself but in a way far worse than the street walker, for what he sells is not his body but his soul.

Selling yourself out also destroys your talent—A writer to make anything of himself must push himself as far as he can go everyday, must choose the highest subject matter, then learn how to present it in a style worthy of the subject matter, taking years to find worthy ideas to write about and the ability to write about them in a worthy way. A writer who sells out cannot reach the highest levels of art when each and every day he lowers himself, for he is not choosing the highest ideals and striving for the highest ideal of style, for such a man his talent being shrunk down cannot enlarge itself enough to embrace greatness.

Think of talent as being like a balloon, it can expand or contract. To make talent expand you have to be pushing it everyday as hard as you can. Everyday that passes where you are not pushing your talent it *contracts*.

He who shrinks his standards down shrinks his talent down, and often finds once he has truly shrunk his talent down it cannot be enlarged ever again.

When the day comes when you demand the best of yourself how can you do the best you are capable of when everyday before that you have been failing to do the best you are capable of?

The writer who strives for only the highest possible standards each and every day enlarges his talent, both in his artistic skill and his spirit, not being deflated by low standards his talent balloons to reach the greatest he is capable of.

Selling yourself out takes the joy out of the creative process—The writer who writes for an audience since he is saying things he does not believe in sees the writing as work to be done for a greater end and not as an end in itself will find no joy from the creative work itself; indeed he will often find only boredom and revulsion at speaking things he does not believe in or care about. Nor will he ever return to the work again for in opening up his own creation only opens up in him a sense of shame and revulsion for his own work openly displays back to him his own corrupt nature.

The writer who speaks his own truths in his own voice finds a joy so great in the creative process itself it is its own end and reward. The writer who finds his joy in the creative process finds whatever he invests into it is paid back to him a million times over, both in the joy of creating it and in the joy of knowing he created it.

For most writers fame is elusive, money more so, so to have a worthwhile career in art you have to find your greatest reward in the joy of creating art. Here by this ideal joy is always to be found, and if money or fame come your way they are small joys which just add to the greater joy of creating art.

Selling out loses the fire—The artist of true integrity who writes only about the great values that fire him up will see his words have the fire in them. The writer who writes for money or fame will lack the passion for the writing itself, and without the passion his writing will always lack the fire.

On the ironic justice for the sell outs—The problem with those who sell out is that in the very act of selling themselves out for fame or fortune it often makes it less likely they will achieve those ends. The lowering of artistic standards in order to appeal to an audience often ensures the artist will not get any recognition, or else a recognition of someone who produces lower quality work; here it is not fame but infamy he receives. The money grubber producing low quality work finds few willing to pay for such low quality work. The ironic justice—the man who alters his art to suit the public taste is the man least likely to appeal to the public taste; this is the consequence of a man who sells himself to the public.

The writer who seeks the widest possible audience often does so by lowering his standards to the lowest common denominator. Here he betrays himself and his art, and in doing makes a work of art unworthy of fame or fortune. Ironically the audience is often turned off by the very lowering of standards. They then grant him not fame but infamy, not fortune but poverty. The audience for an artwork though they themselves as a whole may not hold the highest standards will respond to the higher standards set by others.

The basic problem for those who do not care about their subject matter but pleasing a mass audience is that since they themselves do not understand the importance of meaningful ideas in writing because they lack it in themselves and so cannot write works that truly express meaningful ideas. The man who writes without a deep belief in the moral worth of what he is writing his lack of belief will be reflected back from his pages. The real worth of the art is lost as he uses the form of literature without producing worthy content in it. An audience seeking ideas fails to find it, or seeing it insincerely presented sense the insincerity of the writer presenting it. Insincerity can be smelled even from the pages of a book.

A true sellout cannot emulate a true artist—Sometimes a writer who sells out tries to jump on a higher bandwagon, emulating the success of a classier more talented artist as a way to achieve fame or money or whatever it is besides the actual writing that motivates him. In this case the goal is to copy a work of elevated standards and stature; although the writer himself is morally low his copying of a higher standard will elevate his book over the works designed to appeal to the lowest common denominator, yet the end result will always fall far short of the original. Whenever someone comes out with a new idea or a new ideal of art and achieves success and acclaim there is always a rush by the writing copycats to whore themselves in following the one who first achieved success and acclaim so they can grab their share of it to. The amazing thing about the copycats is always how universally bad the copies are. With the ones who started the crazes their works achieved the success they did because the artist came up with an idea of true worth, and they truly believed in the worth of it, they had some truly important ideas or values to communicate, and they concentrated on bringing their ideas to life, disregarding other factors like fame or money in their passion for their ideas, and their passion worked to bring forth a great artistic work. The copycats lacked the understanding of the true meaning of the original work, copied some of the surface elements of the original, missing the deeper elements that are what actually worked to make the original a success and logically failed to produce anything of value. They miss the deeper meaning because they themselves do not have any understanding of the deeper meaning. The copycats often add in such things as action or romance yet divorced from the meaning which caused them in the original. Action, adventure, romance, sex, drama, etc. all of these things are of little value in books or any artistic medium unless they are attached to some higher meaning. A story devoid of higher meaning no matter how good all of the other elements are will always be an artistic failure if nothing else. Look at the latest Hollywood movies long on action, explosions, violence and naked women but also almost completely lacking in plot, heroes, and truly meaningful values to see what I mean.

Even looking at things from the viewpoint of the bottom line having artistic integrity is often the best way to ensure you profit from what you write. Now the standard of artistic integrity advocated here if followed may seem like it will end up financially crippling the writer, yet this standard while not designed for financial success is often the only means to it. Oftentimes the only way to sell is by not selling out. The great writers in history were always the ones who went their own way and wrote what they wanted to write, which was the most meaningful thing they could write, and oftentimes these were the ones who became successful on multiple levels. The great writers are often the ones who choose to ignore the popular fads or standards of the moment and to blaze their own trails. The writers of integrity do not follow the waves they often create them, and as the first to ride the wave are often the most successful and ride the highest on both the literary and financial levels.

Despite the idea that some artists hold that most men have low tastes in fact the exact opposite is often true; many men have high taste, and will respond to an elevated work of art. The masses are often driven by revulsion away from the very low works deliberately designed to appeal to them. The masses alleged to be inferior in taste in going to artistic works often have higher standards than the ones producing them. Almost all men want a work of art that has some truly deep meaning, not something to pass the time but a book of such value and meaning the book transforms and uplifts them, where the men reading it feel as if they should be in a church while reading a book of such an exalted nature.

On copying others—Many writers sell themselves out by copying other writers, writing as others have been writing not because they believe it is the right way to write but because others do write that way. Here is the problem in copying—lets say you decide to copy Shakespeare, you study him and copy him and maybe in time you even start to sound a little like the bard himself, and in the long run the best outcome is you will only be a second rate copy of Shakespeare, for you will never outdo Shakespeare in being Shakespeare. And even if the impossible does occur and you outdo Shakespeare in being Shakespeare you are still nothing more than a copy of Shakespeare, perhaps a very good copy but still a copy nonetheless. The copier is essentially worthless for he adds nothing new to the world of ideas or art. The world already has his plays, his sonnets, it does not need copies of these works, it needs new ideas spoken in a new voice. All great art has come from a writer speaking his truth in his voice. No great art has ever come from a parrot or its human equivalent.

You can do more than plagiarize an artist's words, you can plagiarize their soul. To copy the spirit of another artist ensures you lose your own spirit and become only a faint echo of his. A slavish copying in practice ends up being a slavish copy in print. In grammar while we all learn the same rules we must learn how to use them in our own way. As an artist you can learn from others how to speak well but always speak in your own voice. In studying other artists learn the principles and techniques that make great writing but learn how to apply them in your own way.

Follow your own genius—let your own genius be enough for it is enough. Let the path to greatness be your path and not treading the well worn path of someone else. The writers who copy others develop only a talent for copying others. Those who copy greatness in the end become only an echo of someone else's greatness. If you free yourself from the need to copy others this allows the realization of your true potential, to not speak as others have spoken but to speak in your own voice and *this* is greatness.

On following tradition—Many follow a dead past, following tradition not because it is good but *because it is tradition*. Some writers follow tradition because they think it will gain them an audience, an audience predisposed to taking what they already know. Some writers follow tradition because to do otherwise means they would have to think for themselves. In blindly following tradition the traditionalist in effect says I will allow others to determine my standards, only those others are not the living but the dead. In following a dead past this denies to you the chance to think as you should in the present. There can be no integrity in blindly following something without any thought as to if it is right to follow it. You can follow a tradition if you think it is right but do not follow a tradition *because* it is a tradition.

In all the great works of art the artist always sets out alone, and usually against all conventional standards, armed with nothing but a great idea and their belief in their idea. They break all known standards and thus move all of art to new higher standards. Tradition is a dead hand which cannot lift anything up. To break with tradition is to raise the chance you can take art to a higher place than where tradition has now placed it.

On committee writing—Now some deal with and allow others to alter or edit their works not as a way to conform or sell out to others but to use others as a way to raise the quality of their own writing. This is what I call committee writing. While the idea may in theory seem good, to try and raise up the quality of the writing thru employing the aid of others, the idea generally backfires in actual practice, because the general nature of committees is that they do not add to the value of the work but instead work to subtract from the strength of the message being presented and thus weaken the work. The more pens writing messages on the page the weaker the overall message becomes. Adding numbers in art subtracts from the value of a work of art, a reverse mathematical process. History shows us that all of the truly great works of literature were produced by single individuals working alone with nothing but their own convictions to guide them. For an example The Gettysburg Address, one of the great speeches of history produced by one man. Nowadays no American president could write such a speech. Why? Because they lack the talent? No! It is because of the *process* presidents use to write speeches, which by using the many ensures the work will be too diluted to have any real worth. Nowadays presidents have committees, many speech writers, use advisors, take polls to decide what should be said, and using all of these methods of using many others to try and write something great ensures that no president will produce a speech that could equal in greatness The Gettysburg Address. The problem with committee writing is that there are too many viewpoints, too many people all speaking their own message their own way making for what could have been one clear message being diluted and downplayed, conflicted and contradicted. Rather then going down one clear track as it would have been if it was guided by one mind clear on where it was going committee writing sees a literary work become like a train derailment, everything going in every direction and nothing going in the right direction.

What if a Shakespeare had submitted his works to committees? Do you think he would be thought of as a literary giant? Do you think we would even be talking about him today? If we did talk of him it would be as an example of how not to write.

Committee writing is not necessarily immoral, unless you allow the committee to express ideals you do not agree with, you can still express worthwhile values through committees only most likely your message will be weakened rather than strengthened by the many.

One strong voice will always be heard more clearly than a mob shouting.

Always fight to ensure that your writing remains exactly that, *YOUR* writing. In the end the literary work and yourself will be better for it.

On artistic competition—Artists are often competitive, and often enter into contests with others, yet artistic competitions generally do not drive artist to higher levels of their art but force them to drive against their own artistic integrity. The artist who competes against others his goal becomes merely to be better than others, not necessarily to be his best. Here his art becomes a sporting event, the art itself secondary to the sport of art. In competition the artist must alter his art to suit the rules of the competition rather than suit his own highest rules. Here the writer sells himself out in order to be seen as better than others rather than following his own standards in order to better himself.

Here is the ideal you should hold on artistic competition—art should not be reduced to a sporting event. I am not in competition with others, I do not compete against anyone, in writing I compete only against myself, to push myself as far as I can go.

On the degradation of pursuing fame—For those who pursue fame what they seek is not actual greatness within themselves but the *appearance* of greatness in the eyes of others. A fame seeker is a person who will often seek the appearance of being something without actually being it. The fame seeker regards what people say of him as of greater importance than what he thinks and is. This is a person who will do or say whatever it takes to make people talk of him, even if he regards it himself as something low and unworthy. What a fame seeker is is nothing more than a drooling dog who will perform in whatever way will make his masters clap and give him the bone of recognition.

The man who sells himself out for fame will find it has little value to him if he achieves it, for the men cheering at him or not cheering him but a false image he has presented to the public. The real truth that he alone carries within him is one that brings shame, for the truth is he is a liar and a whore who sold himself out for fame.

Fame is an afterthought to the true artist. The true artist's thinking is I do not seek fame only to produce great art, and if I ever achieve fame let my seeking and finding of greatness be my only claim to fame and nothing else. Fame should not be the standard of success, at its best let it only be a recognition that some worthy others recognize your worthy success, a recognition all good artist want but will not sell themselves out as artist for.

On writing for a living—Now there are some writers who will say to the standard upheld here that writing is my *occupation,* I write because it is my job to write. The difference between the writers who have integrity in writing and those who sell themselves out for a job lies in the basic spirit of the person and how they approach their writing. Now there are some writers who approach this field as a job, and under such a spirit write to "stay alive". Morally and artistically then these kinds have a mentality of saying through their writing whatever needs to be said so as to obtain their goal, selling themselves out to get by in life, although where they are going in life probably is not really worth it. Those who write just to stay alive will see their writing will just have no life in it. Then there are those who write because they are alive, who are damn glad about it and have something to say about it. Writing becomes a means for them to express the exaltation in living, to capture and express the values that make life worth living for, their writing a joy in and of itself. The spirit of their writing expresses an outpouring of the joy of life. I am alive their words say, and this fact should be sung out in celebration, and this spirit translated into their writing raises it to a level beyond what any writer lacking this spirit and is just writing for a job can hope to obtain even when they try to copy that spirit. A worker drudging away at his job cannot sing the celebration of life; his work at best will have the cadence of a chain gang chanting.

Of these two kinds of artist, those who create to stay alive and those who create because they are alive and want to celebrate it, the two types of art that these kinds will create will be a artwork made from a drudging duty to feed oneself which will reflect the drudgery and a celebration of life artwork which will sing the celebration.

The writing as a job mentality takes the joy out of writing and puts the drudgery in. Here the job standard says do not write for joy but for a paycheck. The standard you should hold—writing for me is not a way to make a living *it is life*. Forget money for life and create art as a means of living life, and in spiritual coin you will become rich beyond measure.

Those who write for money find their passion from art lies in its making money can have no passion for the art or the creating of it. Anyone who spends their time writing works they have no passion for and are even repulsed by to gain money is wasting away something far more valuable than money, they are wasting away the time of their life. If you want money become a businessman. Writing always pays you back but not always in real gold coin but in the golden spiritual coin of joy.

There is nothing wrong with a writer who sells the merits of his work for money but in writing to create works of merit you cannot create them solely for money or sell the merit out for money. You can sell but do not sell out.

While the writer of integrity while in the professional sense it may be "his job" to write he does not approach his writing as a job; he approaches it as an artist regardless of what effect such a context will have on "the job."

Amateur versus professional—The word amateur comes from the

Latin word amore, love. An amateur originally meant someone who did something for the love of it. In this sense all true artist begin and always remain amateurs. (Even if their art pays the bills.)

On writing to serve the public—There are some that regard art as a public service, where the artist writes only to serve the public welfare. Again this is a standard for sellouts for it makes what others think and need of greater importance than what you think and need. The problem with serving a public is what it thinks it needs and what it actually needs are often two different things. Art's concern is not the petty issues of the day but the universal and highest issues which concern all men thru all time. To serve the public you cannot give a damn about the public thinks, instead stay focused on the highest ideas and ideals, and let the public follow you as best it can and here is how you best serve the public; if it keeps up with you then it is worthy of your art and if not then it is not a worthy thing to write for.

Presenting your work to the public—While aware that there are going to be readers of your work you must not consider what they want to hear but only what you want to say, but you must be sure that what you want to say was said *clearly*. In addressing other people what you must do is not act as if you are addressing a mob but a human mind. Frame your ideas in a way in which a mind can see them clearly. This is not selling out but living up to the highest human ideal, the very ideal of what it means to be a human being, *being rational*.

An artist with integrity addresses his work not to an audience but to a human mind. His artistic principles are designed not for the purpose of fame or money but for the purpose of rationality.

To uphold artistic integrity reduce the audience you intend to write for to one—yourself. As far as judging your audience think of yourself as your only audience. Write what you actually want to read. Write it in a way that is appealing to you to read it. When reviewing your writing ask yourself do you like what was written about and how it was written? If yes nothing else need be considered.

This is the ideal artistic integrity brings you to—my pen is the clear expression of my soul, and nothing else.

In the end the only one who has to buy your book is you. As your most important reader and greatest critic you cannot afford your own disapproval.

On publishing—By going against conventional standards and all forms of lowering standards and by going for the highest possible the writer often finds he has to wage a war to ensure his integrity not just in the writing process but also in the publishing process. Integrity in publication means that in bringing your work to the outer world that you allow no one in the outer world to edit, censor, alter, dilute or betray your work and what it stands for. When I say you must not allow others to edit or censor your work what this means is that you must not allow others a power over and above your own rational judgment. You must hold the *final* say. You must hold the authority over your work, both legal and moral, to say if *this* is the way *I think* it should be then *this* is the way it *will* be published. With this standard if your standards and the publisher come into conflict it is the standards which stay and the publisher who goes. You alone must hold the cutting knife of the editor over your work. Allow any others to hold the knife and they will cut out more than parts of your art, they will end up cutting out parts of your soul. Of course if publishers or editors point out errors in what you wrote, grammatical mistakes, superfluous scenes, writing that lacks clarity etc. you may yourself take the editing knife to your work according to their suggestions but *only if you believe* that they are right. The ultimate and only authority over your works must be you and only you. A writer like all moral men should not bow down before other men. A writer should not yield to the force or pressure exerted by other men but what he must yield to is the power of reason. A man though who follows reason is not bowing down but raising himself up to his proper place.

Why publish—The true artist publishes his work to the world because he wants *his ideas* to *live in the world*. The writer does not want to see the value and ideas of his art stand forever apart from and dead to the real world but to become a part of and live in the real world and to give life to the world. A writer publishes as the means to give birth to his ideas in the real world; the ideas once inside of him are through the labor of the writing and publishing process given birth to in the world so they may live outside of him, beyond him, after him.

This is what art does, it preserves ideas in an embryonic form so they may impregnate the reader and be born from him.

The true artist publishes his works for the sake of the ideas in the work. The true value of art lies in the ideas contained within the art.

What a writer wants with money—The true artist does not create art in order to make money; he wants money in order to create art. Money is seen by the true artist as a means to serve the end of art. The greatest thing money can buy you is time. Money to the writer is a means to buy time for himself so he can write full time. Writing does not require a lot of expensive equipment, a pen and some paper and you have all the physical tools needed to write. Even those who go high tech in their writing, meaning those who use computers, need only a small investment to begin writing. What most writers really need to work but that is expensive to buy is time, a large block of time to do the thinking and working that is needed to produce literary works. The need to buy time is the real reason why a writer of integrity wants to make money from his works, so the money can buy him time. To have success in publishing is good for it allows a writer to work *only* as a writer. It frees him from having to work at other jobs to pay the bills, jobs which distract him from the only job that truly matters, the writing. Yet this does not mean a writer should sell himself out for it, because selling out in order to buy time for the writing defeats the whole purpose of writing.

The writer who sells himself to buy his time to be free to write will find that even if he gains enough money to buy his time his time is no longer worth having since he is no longer an artist but a whore who has sold himself and his ideas away for money; he no longer has anything worth saying as an artist and is worth nothing as a human being.

For a writer in love with the art of writing the fruits of his labor lie mostly in the labor itself; to conceive and create an idea in artistic form is the true value and joy of art. The writing life is the life dedicated to ideas. Writing is to him a way of life, the financial rewards of publishing is seen as a way to continue to live the good life of being a writer.

Defining success as a writer—First let us define what it means to be a successful writer—you are a successful writer not when you are published and read by the public but when you write things worth reading. I think of myself as a successful writer whenever I write a sentence worth reading; by this standard almost everyday of my writing career allows me to feel a success. Follow this standard yourself and a lifetime of writing success lies ahead of you. So many writers define success as being published and/or read, and so pursue that standard of success, doing whatever it takes to achieve that success, even if to do so means to sell themselves out as artist. Many in their definition of success define a standard which makes it likely or necessary for them to sell themselves out to achieve that success. Their definition of success lies in dollar signs, or popular reading lists, and not in the value of the art itself. They write to be read rather than to be worth reading, and to do so sell themselves and their ideas out, elevating the idea of success over their own personal and moral ideas. This is why it is important to arrive at a proper perspective on success, so you achieve a worthwhile success rather than an unworthy success.

If in one day you can give birth to a single idea or labor to write one good sentence that holds that idea consider that a successful day and yourself a successful writer.

Realize this truth in the publishing of art—publishers are in it for the money, whereas real artist are in it for the art; this fact leads to inevitable conflict, artistic integrity versus the bottom line. Many publishing houses use an artist eagerness to publish his work to get him to compromise his work, his eagerness "for success" ends up pushing artistic integrity to the wayside to make way for the eagerness. This is why it is so important to approach the publishing process with the right view on success; success is a good work published or not not a compromised work published.

Artistic integrity versus society—Oftentimes an artist will find himself being led into conflict with a far more powerful force than his publisher, the power of society. Society, which can mean governmental censors, courts, ideologically motivated groups, religious authorities etc. such groups who are often dedicated to the halting of free thinking and the repression of man's mind will often try to censor a writer's work because his ways of thinking do not square with theirs. In being in conflict with society a writer will often see the power of society to be turned against him and his art and become a threat to both. Here is where men sellout out of fear. This is a difficult situation for a writer to be in. If a society or government or any form of repressive authority wishes to edit or censor your works the moral thing to do as a true artist is to either defy them or deny them. Depending on the severity of the consequences you can defy them by publishing it anyway in that country choosing the possibility of enduring those consequences. Or defy them by trying to evade the consequences by going around them and doing something like publishing under a pseudonym. Or if there is no way around the consequences and the consequences are too great defy them by fleeing to another country and publish the work. If you live within a country that allows for censorship the best advice is to flee to freer pastures. (If such exists.) In this case you can publish the works without having to become an unnecessary martyr. If you cannot find any way at all around the control of others then the only moral thing to do is deny them by while going on creating works of art not publishing the works at all. Some lacking in a sense of artistic integrity will say to this advice but that defeats the whole purpose of my work. This though is not how a true artist sees things. His purpose in writing is to create the works for himself, because he has important values to express, because he loves the writing process, because he loves to read his own works, because he wants his ideas to live in him. Publishing a work is a secondary benefit when compared to the process of creating it. A chance to share with others, to achieve respect or money, all the benefits that come from publishing while nice benefits only qualify as fringe benefits to the man who sees himself primarily as a creator. The one thing that is not an option is to neither defy or deny the censorship but to accept it.

As possible censorship in a society should be defied; an act that benefits both the artist and the society, freeing both the artist and the society from the realm of brute force to the realm of ideas. No society has even benefited from throttling the human mind. If you wish to benefit society then stop giving a damn about it and follow your mind to whatever truths it can find and society will benefit in the end from gaining whatever truths your free thinking mind found.

Now some writers sell out not to a physical or violent force from society but from the peer pressure of society, where they fear being morally condemned by society overall; they sell out not to any actual physical pressure but to what they perceive as the pressure that may be exerted by other men's denouncements or ridicule. Here other men's looks, tone of voice, snide comments, etc. become a horrific monster to be feared and bowed down to. If a man is wrong to sell out to the threat of jail, torture or death how much lower is the man who sells out to a snooty tone of voice? In this case the writer in his mind builds up this monstrous entity known as society, he looks at what all other men are doing and follows what they are doing, afraid to stand up to a pressure which does not really even exist except in his head. This is a man guided by a herd mentality; he is a coward who is so afraid of others he betrays himself out of fear the herd may moo disapprovingly at him.

The ultimate consequence of selling out—Perhaps the worst consequence of all of selling out is that the sellout pays for it in guilt. The knowledge he is a sellout haunts him. Any coin he receives is tinged with the rust of guilt, any applause the mockery of his shame. Any mention or sight of his book brings him revulsion; he literally has to turn and flee from the sight of his own work.

Whatever you do do not sell yourself out through the selling of your writing. Do not turn your writing into a guilt inducing experience. Even if by selling out you achieve fame or money every ounce of recognition and every penny you receive is not a payment to you but something you pay for in guilt. There are better ways to live life and make a living than by prostituting your soul. In selling out you lose the true values of writing, and find that in obtaining the very things you sold out for that such outer goals actually become not a source of pleasure but a source of pain and regret.

Do not seek greatness in the eyes of others; seek greatness in your own eyes. Value what you think above what others think. Place a high enough value on yourself as an artist and as a human being to think for yourself and be yourself and to not serve as a mouthpiece for others in order to get those others to mouth off about you. Let any fame that comes your way be from a worthy recognition, let others say here is a man who lives up to his standards, and his standards are the highest possible, and let any fame that comes from this be a fringe benefit of men recognizing what you already know, that you are a good artist and more importantly a good human being. Let any coin that comes your way not be darkly tinged with the rust of guilt, for you cannot afford to pay the price for that.

The artist as hero—The artist becomes heroic when he follows his vision no matter how many obstacles he comes up against and ends up going over those obstacles to present his vision to the world *uncompromised.*

It can often be a heroic struggle for an artist to end up presenting his artistic vision without any compromise. As the world of art is always under siege by the forces of compromise, a siege in which so many end up surrendering, the few artists who emerge with their vision uncompromised are truly heroes.

Only the ideal of artistic integrity can keep an artist true to his vision, for it is the wall that protects him from the siege of compromise.

The artist is a hero whenever he says what needs to be said regardless of what anyone says about it.

There is nothing good that is going to come from morally compromising yourself. Know this truth and it makes it easy to find the hero within you.

Follow your truth no matter how far from the crowd it takes you. All great truths were first discovered by the one person who had the courage to break from the crowd. Be a daredevil in thought. Take great leaps. Do not fear crashing; better a sincere crash than an insincere success.

IDEALISM

The true artist sets off alone, with nothing but his own goal to set his course, nothing but his own artistic ideals to guide him, nothing but belief in the righteousness of his vision moves him. With this ideal as his moral compass the true artist is the Columbus of ideas, new ways to new lands, his lands, a new paradise on earth he discovers and gives to all of us.

The artist kingdom is always under siege by the forces of compromise. Here in this essay I have sought to give you the defenses (ideas) to protect your artistic kingdom. And those who do endure the siege and triumph over it find themselves reigning over a great and glorious kingdom, as opposed to those who gave in and see their kingdom looted of all its worth by the barbarians of compromise.

The ultimate consequence of not selling out—To be an artist guided by the principle of artistic integrity finds this strict standard first elevates you as an artist, both in what you write and how you write it. It expands the spirit of your writing, uplifts the nature of what you are writing about and causes your talent to expand to the levels needed to reach your high ideals. To write guided by the ideal of artistic integrity ensures that you at least reap the greatest and most important reward of writing, the joy of engaging in artistic creation. And as you climb ever higher, guided solely by the standard of going for the highest possible to man you will in fact reap fame and money as other men cheer you on. Most important of all you raise himself up as a human being by making your art and your whole life a dedication to the highest possible to man.

8

The Writer's Toolkit

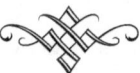

Writing is word construction, of putting words together in a certain way to achieve a certain desired result or effect. In great writing words and sentences are built together in a soaring structure building upwards to an intellectual and emotional climax; when we read such well constructed structures the words work themselves into us and they become a part of us. This happens only when a writer employed the right literary tools, those that enabled him to build up to something truly powerful and awe inspiring in his writing.

The power possessed by those who can construct great structures with words is immense. The right construction of words has the power to bring joy to the heart, healing to the soul, wisdom to the mind, and uplift the human spirit.

Yet not all constructions of words move men, or move in the way intended. Sometimes by an ill construction of words we move men in ways we did not intend, to revulsion, to contempt, to laughter, or worst of all, boredom.

The writer is a word architect; with words he constructs works of art. A writer uses words to build up to something. Words like a building can soar, shelter, close off, repulse or even collapse in upon itself.

Good writing builds up to a stunning effect. Good writing in each word, sentence, paragraph, builds on itself and adds to a growing sum.

Good writing affects the reader in some way, where when done reading he says to himself yes *that* was *worth* reading.

In this part we discuss the nuts and bolts of writing, the techniques upon which great literary structures are built. A writer should hold a list of techniques he can employ in his sentences or paragraphs so they build upwards to something great. All great writers should have a writer's toolkit, a series of ideas on how to present ideas; a series of literary tools which structure words in a certain way to build up to a certain effect.

The following is a series of literary techniques or tools a writer can employ to create powerful structures of writing. These are not ideas that must be employed at all times they are merely tools to be used when you believe they will help you to build up to something magnificent in your writing.

Plot tools

1—*A bold beginning*—One should never build boredom thru words, or create throw away writing, words meant to be forgotten, or employ a form of writing that allows the readers attention to wander at any point in a written work, but the avoidance of disposable or boring writing becomes of paramount importance in the opening of a work. The opening of a written work is the time to grab the reader's attention and not let go, for this may be the only time to grab his attention. Use a bold arresting beginning as a means to grab attention. In the very beginning of a work make a startling assertion, reveal a stunning fact, ask an intriguing question, raise a mystery, state a high ideal, express joy or some other high emotion. A powerful opening tends to lead to a powerful follow through. Do not waste an opening on insipid pleasantries, or relating unimportant information. Open powerfully, and you will grab hold of the reader and keep him. A powerful opening leads to a powerful desire to read on and find out what that opening leads to.

For an example if writing about the effects of cancer and how it is a monumental killer one way to catch the reader's attention might be to reveal a stunning fact by opening this way, "Here I seek to warn you about the largest mass murderer now stalking the land, cancer."

2—*Start with the climax*—Most books follow this progression, 1—opening, 2—middle section, 3—climax, 4—closing. The problem with this is you have to build up to the interesting parts, the build up taking the chance of building up boredom. Instead of following the old standard progression start the book off with your climax—for example if writing a murder mystery start the book off with the murder occurring and then flash back to the events which caused it to occur. Starting with the climax will make readers want to know how you got there. Starting with the climax colors your work with the spirit of mystery. The reader is moved further into your work thru curiosity.

3—*State the bottom line first line*—In your work state the whole meaning of the work in the first line or as close to it as you can get, and sum your work's meaning in a single sentence, or as few sentences as possible. Make your meaning or goal as clear as possible as soon as possible. Give the reader a standard to refer right at the beginning which guides him to the end. For example if your goal is to argue for freedom and you are doing so by arguing against governmental controls reveal this fact right in the beginning, saying this book is for freedom and against any form of tyranny over man.

4—*Ask questions*—To point blank assert something upon the reader, to say you must think this, or you must accept this, is to take a chance you will turn the reader off, and certainly such a style does little to turn the mind on, since there is nothing offered to be thought about. Use questions which provoke thought. A question forces a mind to begin thinking rather than passively accepting. Use a question in a way which will cause the reader to give the answer which proves your position. Sometimes the best teachings come in the form of questions. For example "How can you gain the world when you have lost your mind?" The idea of the importance of the integrity of the mind is stated in the form of a question which if men answer correctly will make them accept the idea. Each man must make his own journey to the truth. Arriving at an answer always means more when it is *our* answer, even if it is someone else who started us on the journey to that answer.

5—*State consequences*—Rather than a bland stating of your position instead list the consequences that justify the position you wish to stand for. Here is an example of how you can use a listing of consequences to make an anti-war statement. Rather than using a self-righteous statement such as 'I am against this war' instead state it like this, "This current foreign policy has killed hundreds of thousands of innocent men, emptied our treasury, lost our civil and personal liberties, lost our decency, lost our allies, made our old enemies more determined and made us many new determined enemies, with no success yet and with the looming certainty that there will never be any success." This statement not only states your position without being self-righteous it also leaves your opponents with nothing to stand on.

6—*The tower of facts*—To make a point pile up your evidence in a series of single sentences or sections numbering them, building up a tower of them to the point where no sane person could reject your point if they accept your evidence for it. For example if you are against a foreign war state your reasons why it is bad in a 1, 2, 3, etc format, and as you reach 10, 20, 30 etc. the building up of the towering argument of reason becomes impossible for any *rational* person to ignore or reject.

7—*Character opposition*—Put opposing characters into your works. Use this not just as a means to create action but as a way to show two sides of the issue. Opposing characters allows for a reader to see multiple perspectives. The contrast creates the drama, not just physical but also more importantly spiritual.

8—*Entering into a character*—More than just showing the actions of a character enter into the consciousness of the character to show *why* he is taking them. This psychic entry is one of the greatest powers of literary art over other art forms, it can enter into a person. Do not just skim the surface of a character, go into the depths of him.

9—*Give small things great meaning*—Attach the small things and random events that happen in life to some profound lesson or deeper meaning for life. Go from small events to wide scale meanings. Attach seemingly insignificant details to some philosophy or principle. Even the smallest of events can have the greatest of meaning. A sun rising can be just a sun rising or a religious event; writing about a sunrise can be a way to teach us how to see it as a religious event.

10—*Story time*—Sometimes even the best theoretical discussion can fail to fully illustrate the meaning of something so instead illustrate your meaning with a story. You can make up a story, use someone else's story or use real events. A story often has a far greater effect than abstract discussion would have for here we see the consequences played out in front of us rather than merely being told of them.

11—*Use epic plots*—The greater the value pursued the greater the conflict it demands. Make your plot one with values which are worthy of being pursued in it; make your pursuit epic enough for the values being pursued. No easy adventures for great treasure. Love that comes easy is not worth writing about. In the fight for a great value minor conflict will not do; no small battles for great values; great values demand great battles. Idealism demands the epic.

12—*Fill in your world with details*—In creating a literary world, particularly one that is set in another world as in science fiction or in another time delve into the many small details of that world. The details of a world create the atmosphere which is what the characters and readers breathe in, making them a part of that world. Not every detail included must be so for it moves the plot along, a lot of times good writers include many details to create an atmosphere, so you are moved into it and can see and understand the world the character is moving in.

13—*Time travel*—Use flashbacks. To go from the present to the past, to time travel in a book, is a common literary technique for it is often the past which determines the present. You can time travel thru chapters, even in a single paragraph.

14—*A timeless work*—In writing a story if possible do not set it in any specific time or place. A work devoid of timely details such as dress, manners, technology, instead focuses the work back onto the characters and ideas they hold. A timeless work shows the universality of human experience, that regardless of whether we are wearing an animal skin, a toga or modern dress we all have the same nature, deal with the same issues, feel the same things, even if wearing different forms of dress in doing so. A timeless work can focus away from the minutia of daily life to the most fundamental issues of human life.

15—*Letter writing*—In addressing the world use the technique as if you are writing a private letter, allowing you to speak in a personal tone which in any other format would be unseemly but seems fine in the letter format. Letter writing often allows for a more intimate style and feeling. Here you address the reader not as an impersonal subject but as if he were a close friend.

Style tools

1—*Use power words*—Use words which in and of themselves can achieve an effect. Use the word defiance instead of against. Use thunderous rather than loud. Say I felt exalted rather than I felt sort of good. If there was a bloody battle do not say there was some blood spilt say the fields turned red with the blood of men. Use power words as appropriate to evoke images, to stir men's spirits, to create a more powerful effect. Power words both make the reader more interested in the idea being spoken of so powerfully and make him more inspired to accept the idea. Power words hit the reader hard, breaking thru his personal defenses and entering right into the deepest part of his being.

2—*Make the abstract concrete*—The biggest problem in explaining an abstraction is that the reader often cannot see thru the label to see what you actually mean, so make all abstractions concrete—to describe evil and give us an idea of what it is you can describe it as being like cockroaches, the many who are small, disgusting and run at the sight of anything human, which draws an image of the abstract concept of evil. Use visual imagery to describe the abstract.

3—*Use symbolism*—Employ everyday objects to symbolize a greater meaning. A veil can be more than a veil, it can mean hidden desire, repression, secrecy and all of these things and more together. Imbue mundane objects with deep meaning. This is using word-painting to add depth, one visual image leading to other deeper visual images.

4—*Microscoping*—Use sentences with a microscopic focus on details. For example do not just say 'he was wearing a flannel shirt', for that tells us little, say 'he was wearing a worn flannel shirt, smudged with paint, smelling of tobacco, its edges frayed from working hard construction.' Here in this example the detailed word-painting of the shirt tells us many things about the person wearing it.

5—*Go from labels into the parts*—Refer to a part or attributes of the thing you are describing rather than the thing itself. For example describe a dog as an over exuberant golden ball of fuzz. This tool gives more depth to your word-paintings.

6—*Use sound symbolism*—The use of sound symbolism is making up words to describe sounds. (Bzzzzz, whoosh etc.) This often makes a style more fun and exuberant.

7—*Let the idea determine the form*—Let the nature of the idea determine the nature of the form you will use. To describe a gentle flowing stream requires gentle flowing words. No harsh or abrupt forms when writing of a gentle stream. To describe a crashing wave requires crashing jarring words, white foam and a more chaotic style. To describe a drummer use a rat a tat tat style. The nature of the style must match the nature of the idea.

8—*Use wit (but not jokes)*—Add wit as appropriate if it works to clarify meaning or else emphasize a point. Do not use jokes in writing like did you hear the one about the rabbi, the priest and the nun. Those kinds of jokes belong only in joke books, never in serious literature. Vulgar humor does not turn on but disgusts and turns off the worthy reader. Humor when inappropriate often ensures that the reader even if he starts laughing stops taking you seriously. Clever wit while it may make a person laugh out loud also at the same time is making his brain work and so he will take what you are saying seriously. Wit is a humorous but also clever use of words used to make a worthwhile point. Vulgar jokes have little humor, nothing clever, and make no worthwhile point.

9—*Pair opposites*—Use words which have the exact opposite meaning of one another in a sentence. For example—"If we do not learn from the past the future will be lost." Pairing opposites is an interesting literary technique for we see paired two words not normally associated with one another.

10—*Use phase reversal*—In constructing a sentence divide it into two halves, and then in the second half use the same words you used in the first half but in reverse order. For example—"When the going gets tough the tough get going." This style of writing easy to remember sticks in the mind.

11—*Pair contradictions*—Put words whose meanings are contradictory together to form a new meaning. For example say he was amazingly average. We remember the contradiction because it is a contradiction.

12—*Use neologisms*—This is putting together two words to make a new word. This is mixing the old to make something new. For example in describing a bureaucrat who is acting like a tyrant describe him as a tyrocrat.

13—*Come at it from many angles*—Sometimes to defeat our opponent and make our point we have to attack his position from many points simultaneously. For example Thomas Paine in talking about the British government and how it was unfit to govern America any more made his point this way, "After the coolest of reflections in the matter *this must* be allowed, that Britain was too jealous of America, to govern it justly; too ignorant of it, to govern it well; and too distant from it, to govern it at all." Here you can see Paine coming at the idea of the unfitness of the British government to govern America by adding many differing points all at once on why this was so.

14—*Use repetition of a word*—Sometimes repeating the same word over and over again can really hammer a point home. For example Thomas Paine in his great political pamphlet Common Sense in talking about reasons why America should declare independence from Britain and how attachment to her drew America into foreign conflicts wrote, "We have boasted the protection of Great Britain, without considering, that her motive was *interest* not *attachment*; that she did not protect us from *our enemies* on *our account*, but from *her enemies* on *her account*, from those who would have no quarrel from us on any *other account*, and who will always be our enemies on the *same account*." Note how repeated use of the word account helps to make men realize that attachment to Britain was only drawing America into unnecessary foreign conflicts.

15—*Create new words*—If the language is inadequate to your means make it adequate. Invent new words; create new meanings for old words. This ideal is not a violation of language it is the very source of language. Language came about because someone somewhere created the words necessary to meet his needs.

16—*Use adjectives to add color and form*—A noun by itself is not a distinct entity until adjectives are added giving to it a distinct form and color. Adjectives are the way of giving color to black and white nouns.

Some writers say to distrust adjectives. I say trust in adjectives, trust that they have a very important place in your writing and trust yourself to know that place. There is no exact rule about the number of adjectives you can use. For example a liberal use of adjectives may not weigh your sentences down but serve as the foundation upon which your ideas are raised up to be presented *clearly* to the world. The use of many adjectives works when they work together, the sum becoming greater than its parts and achieving a powerful effect. Allow adjectives to pile up if their use increases effect, cut them only when they detract or add nothing to the effect.

17—*Use aphorisms*—Aphorisms are short terse statements, a single sentence or two. Aphorisms are short expressions of basic truths. *Aphorisms are the flash of insight.* Aphorisms are a minimum of words used for maximum effect. Aphorisms because of their very shortness are easily held onto for their very shortness. Aphorisms are for those who favor precise clear thought. Aphorisms should fall like lightning, a quick bolt of light and then a tremendous thunder that reverberates within the soul. Aphorisms are often the storm troopers of truth, they make the first assault forcing the reader to surrender and accept their truth, opening up the way for accepting a large body of theory flowing from that first truth.

Aphorisms are suited to the fast pace of life. Brief lines for accelerated thinking, the aphorisms very simplicity makes it easy to apply to life.

The elements of an aphorism—1—short (one to two sentences at the most) 2—no frills (no preface, apologies, messing around) 3—to the point (purest simplest expression of an idea's meaning) 4—declarative (asserts, it does not argue or question or qualify) and 5—universal (wisdom of ages.)

Mind tools

1—*The great opening salvo repeated*—A writer often tries to give the opening of a piece a great wallop, a virtuoso display to start things off with a great bang and then he allows the intensity of his literary assault to level off. In your writing assault do not level off, go full force the whole way thru. Try and write each section as if it were the opening. Approach each section as if it were your one and only chance to catch someone's attention. Nothing mundane, no trivialities, no small firecrackers, only great explosions.

In trying to write each section as it if were the opening you will often end up with a skeletal structure which will need to be fleshed out but what a structure to build with.

2—*Write from a state of being*—To add into emotion into your work you should write from an emotional state. Try in writing an emotion to actually feel the emotion you are writing about when writing. Writing from the feeling will give your work that feeling. If writing about something that outraged the character do not write from a calm state write from a feeling of outrage. In putting in a scene where the character feels the emotion of outrage try to remember something that outraged you in order to actually feel the emotion of outrage, and then write what you are feeling. To try and write a scene of anger feel anger. If writing about love feel love. This is why it is best to write what you know. To write from an emotional state of being you must have felt the emotion.

To try and write a scene of anger from a state of calm contentment means now you are only seeing words, you are not trying to describe something specific to you but a general vague thing, not feeling the anger and seeing what caused it, and so your words will be devoid of feeling.

Do not in doing this switch off your intellectual mind. The intellectual mind is to be used to find the words to describe the feelings, but it is working from something known within and not trying to describe the unknown. When writing from the unknown you are just shooting out a wild guess and often your works will miss the mark of truth.

3—*Create an atmosphere*—Create an atmosphere when writing that is appropriate to what you are writing. For example when writing about romance create a romantic setting to write in. Dim the lights, get some roses, light some candles, and see how such an atmosphere helps to set you in the right mood for writing about that subject.

4—*Steal a life*—Take inspiration for the lives of your characters from the lives of those around you. Taking inspiration from everyone around you opens up the whole range of human nature for you to explore. The artist in and of himself is too limited a thing to draw on for art, for no one holds the whole range of human characteristics within themselves. Let every person you come into contact with be fodder for your art. Every person is a lesson in human nature.

5—*Flesh out your characters*—In creating a character define fully what that character is. In notes define all his essential characteristics, his traits, tastes, principles, personality etc. You must know your character fully if you are to create him realistically on the page. Define your character so fully you know what he would say in real life if he were a real life.

Define your character *beyond* what you need for the story. Create a childhood for a fully grown man. Create a philosophy for the character even if the character will never express it in the story. Although the reader may not need to know the basic essence of a character you the writer should, because everything the character does comes from that essence.

Write outside the story. Write events which you do not intend to put into the story but which help you understand the acts and actions which caused your character to become what he is.

6—*Character possession*—When writing enter into the mind of a character so deeply you see things as he sees them. You begin to think and act (on paper) as he would. A lot of times when you are possessed by a character you leave behind your personal preconceptions and begin to think instinctively as he would and dialogue and acts are written out as the character would have done so in real life.

PERSONAL TOOLS

To perfect your writing skills it is sometimes not enough to just write, you must practice in the art of writing. Sometimes a writer needs specific writing exercises in order to perfect specific talents. Practice may not make perfect but there is no perfection without practice.

The following is a list of writing and personal exercises you can do to improve your ability to write. Writing exercises are useful tools for honing your talent because they can build new tools of thinking into you, or they can be used to sharpen the tools you had which had grown dull. Writing exercises are particularly good tools for beginning writers in helping to teach them the basics of their craft. Writing exercises can also be useful even for you experienced writers, to teach you new lessons or to help you remember old lessons you have forgotten about or else to just help you get out of a rut.

There are two lists of exercises. The first list presents a series of writing exercises you apply to your writing. The second list presents a series of personal exercises you apply to yourself to make yourself better able to write. As how well or poorly you write is often determined by your state of mind or mood good or bad writing sessions can often be the result of something that happened before you even sat down to write. The personal exercises are designed to help ensure that you sit down in the proper state of mind for writing.

Writing exercises

1—*Keep a journal*—Buy a notebook and use it to record your thoughts, ideas, questions, goals, feelings, etc. In this journal do not edit yourself, just let things pour out of you. The value of journal writing is it is a way to learn about yourself, to let the stored up well of your consciousness flow freely and see what is in there. A personal journal often grasps things you rarely touch upon. Some of the things you write about can be used as ideas for future writing projects.

2—*Try to write the perfect sentence or paragraph*—Pick a subject then try and write only one sentence or paragraph on it, writing and rewriting it until you get it absolutely perfect. This teaches you both what the perfect sentence or paragraph is and how to construct them.

3—*Write one page on one subject*—Pick a subject and write a page or two on it. Make sure to limit yourself to a certain amount of space, as a newspaper editorialist would be. The goal of this exercise is to teach you how to choose only the most important things to say when your space is limited. This exercise also teaches you the art of editing, of how to cut out the insignificant and how to know what is the truly significant.

4—*Write about one subject many different ways*—Take an event like a rainstorm and write about it in different ways, as being happy, ominous, dreary, uplifting, dangerous etc. This exercise will help teach you how to project different types of moods.

5—*Use sentence stems*—Start with an incomplete sentence and try to write a paragraph or even an essay from it. For example when I saw the sun rise I __. This exercise teaches you how to write about different subjects.

6—*Create ideal character*—You must learn how to create heroes if you want to learn how to create art worth reading. On paper do a character sketch of what you would define as the ideal human being. Describe everything about him, what he looks like, what he acts like, what he believes in, his moral principles, his tastes, etc. This exercise helps to teach you about characterization and in the most important way possible, on how to create ideal human beings. (This can also be used for personal inspiration for yourself, as an ideal you should measure up to.)

7—*Create the vilest villain*—Since most fiction writing requires villains as foils for the heroes you need to learn how to create villains. Try on paper to create the most loathsome villain you can. As with the ideal character exercise describe every detail about him, what he would look like, what he acts like, what he believes in or why he does not believe in anything, his principles or lack of them, his tastes or his lacking thereof etc. Try to create different types of villains: brutish, suave, smart, dumb etc.

8—*Create plot outlines*—Sit down and devise many different plot outlines for books. Spend a week on this and create twenty or more outlines for short stories and novels. Each plot outline should only be one to a few pages. Study each outline when done and see if it would have the potential to be made into a good book. Some would be good book ideas, others not. Study the good and the bad and think about what separates the two.

Personal exercises

1—*Experience life*—A writer to be able to write about life must actually get out and experience life. To be able to write about things the writer must know what he is writing about. A writer cannot write honestly about what he doesn't know. A virgin should never write a sex scene. To write *convincingly* about a baseball game the writer must know what it is like to step up to the plate and take a swing. The writer must truly get out into life in order to be able to write truly about it. The writer to even have things to write about must be adventurous. How are you to know what is possible in life unless you get out and experience all that is possible in life? The writer should get out into the world and throw himself into adventure, challenge, excitement, romance. The writer should climb mountains, run with the bulls, surf mighty waves, be swept away by love, go out into the world and experience all life has to offer, then throw all life has to offer into his books. As a personal exercise try out new things as material and inspiration for your art.

2—*Pay attention*—Be focused on the world going on around you. Such focus will teach you how to pay attention to the details. Details can be important in a writer's work. Minor details in a story for instance create atmosphere, define characters, create settings etc. Paying attention to all of life's little details also helps you to get ideas for stories. As a personal exercise try noticing the small things and details of things, people's foibles, ways of speaking, funny incidents etc. and try putting these things into your art.

3—*Question the world around you*—Question everything. The journey to truth always begins in a question. Art must express truth. A good writer should never stop questioning the world around him. A childlike curiosity often moves the writer. Curiosity is the key which opens the door to wisdom. The writer seeks the truth of the world around him, to express those truths and to use those truths to find higher truths.

4—*Live your ideas*—A writer should live his ideas. The writer should know if the ideas he believes in and writes about are any good. Communism would have never come into being if its advocates had actually been forced to live their ideal. Before putting an idea to paper put the idea to the test of reality and see if it works in reality.

5—*Let the imagination run wild*—The writer to be able to create must unleash the imagination and let it run loose; for the human imagination once set loose will find whole new worlds. If art is a flight into fantasy then the artist without imagination has no wings to artistically soar on. The writer without imagination cannot find new worlds, he can find nothing new and exciting. The writer who is not the imaginative type should make himself so. If you cannot imagine creatively how can you write creatively? The writer must imagine people unlike any around him, of adventures not yet taken, of worlds which do not (yet) exist, and create these visions on paper so the reader or perhaps the writer himself can make what was just imagination reality.

What is writing but paper catching a writer's imagination? The person who cannot lose themselves in their imagination should probably not become an artist, for the artist must see not just what is but what can be. The writer loses himself in worlds never before seen, as a means to create literary worlds which did not exist before he imagined them. Let your imagination run wild; who knows what world of undiscovered ideals it might find?

6—*Study other art forms*—Study other forms of art, such as sculpture, painting, dance and music; study the *principles* behind these forms of art, see if any of the principles are applicable to your own form of art. Study other art forms and use them for inspiration. Pictures of the Sistine Chapel can be used as source of inspiration to show you what one man is capable of.

7—*Inspire yourself*—Find paintings, movies, music, or anything which works to inspire you with the right attitude. For example if writing a story about heroes watch movies with heroic characters in it before writing as a way to inspire yourself.

8—*Meditate*—Use meditation as a way to focus your mind on your work. Meditation is particularly useful before writing, particularly when your mind is thinking of many other different things when it should be now thinking of only one thing, the writing. Use meditation not to stop thinking but as a way to clear your mind for thinking and thinking only about writing.

9—*The invigorating walk*—Take the dog out if you have one and take a long invigorating walk before writing. In walking the heart is pumping, the body is invigorated, the senses are open, the mind is receiving, the thoughts are flowing. A long brisk walk early in the morning, particularly on a early spring or summer day when it is going to be perfect day out, will oftentimes so inspire and invigorate you that it will double not only your zest for writing but your zest just for being alive and this as a result will improve many times over the quality of your writing. Walking stimulates the body and the mind.

10—*Live healthy*—A healthy lifestyle works to create greater energy and zest for living, such things working to create a more positive mental attitude which will be translated into your work. Healthy living also works to eliminate disease and pain and the resulting states of anxiety and depression they lead to, working to ensure that such attitudes do not interfere with or become a part of your writing. The writer should strive to remain healthy in body. To be healthy in body helps you to be healthy in spirit. A healthy body is free from pain and flowing with energy, a body that sends only good feelings to the spirit, and this encourages the spirit to send out good feelings into the art. Disease, lethargy, pain, these elements either stop the writing process or worse become reflected in the writing process, the writer suffering from something often makes his writing reflect what he is feeling, and his writing becomes a source of pain.

11—*Steer clear of alcohol and drugs*—A classic image of the writer is of him as a hard drinker. Let this image be reframed as the anti-literary image. The image of the hard drinking writer has caused great harm to the literary cause, for a hard drinker is not a hard writer. No writer can write when drunk, and most can barely write when hung over. Alcohol is not an aid to the creative process; it hinders it if it does not stop it completely. The writer should get drunk only on words. The writer should let writing be his high, and if he tries to replace it with a liquid or powdery high he would find his depressed and whacked out mind losing its ability to get high from the writing or to even do the writing.

As a artistic, personal and moral exercise avoid altogether or else severely limit drugs and alcohol, and never ever allow any indulgence to interfere with your writing.

12—*Read the best*—Take the books you think are the best written and study them to figure out what makes them the best. What is it about them that elevates them over the other works out there? The goal in reading the best is not to then go and copy the best but to learn about the principles which made the best the best and to copy those principles in your own writing.

13—*Read the worst*—For the same reasons in reverse study the worst books you ever read. Decide what made them so bad and then consciously avoid emulating the practices and principles which made them so bad in your own writing.

14—*Expand your vocabulary*—The dictionary is a treasure trove of words. The English language has over five hundred thousand words in it, and most people know only a few thousand. This is bad for anyone to be cut off from so many rich and useful words but it is particularly bad for a writer since his occupation in life is employing words. Read a dictionary. Each night before going to bed read a page, or try to learn a new word every day. Make this your motto—a life dedicated to the written word and the written word dedicated to life.

15—*Reward yourself*—When you have completed some work or project reward yourself in some way for doing the work. Do something like go out to eat, or go to the movies. If possible pick a reward like getting a book on writing that helps you to become a better writer.